'Powerful behavioural insights! A practical read for both established and aspiring leaders.'

Dr. Mark Little, Executive Director, Scouts Canada

'A practical, scientific approach to increasing your power and influence in the workplace.'

Dr. Tanya Jenkin, Contractor to Department of Defence, Australia

'A book I wish I'd read 20 years ago!'

Dr. Carlos Costa-Posada, Former Minister for the Environment, Colombia

'A long-overdue revision of the principles of influence for a global audience.'

Dr. Deirdre O'Leary, Executive Director, Abu Dhabi National Oil Company, UAE

'Read this engaging book to accelerate and amplify your influencing skills.'

Dr. Darren Moppett, Global Innovation Director, Procter & Gamble, UK

'Simple, practical, and effective steps for building influence.'

Dr. Mukul Kumar, Chief Innovation Officer, Hult International Business School, Switzerland

ABOUT THE AUTHOR

Dr Amanda Nimon-Peters is a Professor of Leadership at Hult International Business School (Dubai & San Francisco campuses). She is an expert on the use of behavioural science to develop measurable leadership capability, drawing on her significant experience in executive roles as well as her academic expertise. Dr Nimon-Peters spent more than a decade at Procter & Gamble across Europe and the Middle East where she was responsible for recruitment interviewing, people management and successful business delivery. She launched a start-up in Dubai and gained repeat business from international clients such as Cisco, LG Electronics and HSBC. Today she works with multinational companies aiming to improve employee performance, as well as DBA and MBA students seeking to dramatically increase their career success. She holds a PhD from the University of Cambridge, and a First-Class Honours Degree in Psychology from the University of Adelaide. Outside of work, she has completed Ironman and half-Ironman races, and was elected the sixth female member of the British Antarctic Club, following three expeditions spent in a field camp on the Antarctic Peninsula.

Working With Influence

Nine Principles of Persuasion to Accelerate Your Career

Dr. Amanda Nimon-Peters

BLOOMSBURY BUSINESS
LONDON • OXFORD • NEW YORK • NEW DELHI • SYDNEY

BLOOMSBURY BUSINESS
Bloomsbury Publishing Plc
50 Bedford Square, London, WC1B 3DP, UK
29 Earlsfort Terrace, Dublin 2, Ireland

BLOOMSBURY, BLOOMSBURY BUSINESS and the Diana logo are trademarks
of Bloomsbury Publishing Plc

First published in Great Britain 2022

A catalogue record for this book is available from the British Library

Library of Congress Cataloguing-in-Publication data has been applied for

ISBN: 978-1-4729-8873-7; eBook: 978-1-4729-8876-8

4 6 8 10 9 7 5 3

Typeset by Deanta Global Publishing Services, Chennai, India
Printed and bound in Great Britain by CPI Group (UK) Ltd, Croydon CR0 4YY

MIX
Paper | Supporting
responsible forestry
FSC® C171272

To find out more about our authors and books visit www.bloomsbury.com and
sign up for our newsletters

Contents

Introduction: How to Use This Book

Executive summary

Every minute you are awake your perceptions, decisions and behaviour are shaped by multitudes of factors in your mental and physical environments. Most of these effects occur without your conscious awareness, and you might even be shocked to know they exist. Despite their mostly hidden nature, these effects can be detected through studies from psychology and other forms of behavioural science. Very occasionally, with the right perspective, it is possible to glimpse some of these factors at work in your daily life.

This book provides deep insight into the nine principles of influence that affect people's behaviour and decisions most frequently in the work environment. All nine principles are based on robust behavioural science conducted with diverse samples of people from around the world. Each chapter is structured similarly: first, a simple overview of the science, followed by examples and exercises for applying that specific principle in your own professional environment. Each chapter ends with a 'key takeaway' summary.

Like all complex skills, influence can be learned. Your performance will improve the more you practise. You can choose to work with just one principle on its own, or you can attempt to apply the principles in combination. To start learning actionable insights for increasing your personal influence in both face-to-face and virtual workplaces, you need only choose the chapter that interests you most and start practising today.

How much can I expect to improve?

The number one factor that prevents you from improving your skill in influencing others is the belief that you are already good at it. After all, you may have done well in life until now. You might even remember several incidents in which you were charming, clever, and influential – when things turned out in your favour.

Unfortunately, mild to moderate success is often a key factor that prevents people from improving. This is because failure is more conspicuous than the absence of success. When we fail to achieve a desired outcome, that failure is usually obvious. Failure can help us learn what went wrong. In contrast, lack of success is not obvious. If you attend a meeting or a networking event, have a generally agreeable time and chat to a few important people, then nothing went wrong, so what is there to learn? In fact, because of the mechanisms through which we learn new behaviour, so long as our current approaches result in positive outcomes – 'positive' here meaning the absence of obvious failure – then the behavioural patterns we use today only become more likely to be the same approaches we use again in the future. What we do not see is how much more successful we might have been, had we had done something differently.

Now that you have this book in your hands, you have a choice. You can thank your aunt for the present, put it on your desk and use it as a coffee mat so your mug does not leave a stain. You can read it, perhaps enjoy yourself, and feel smart about knowing more stuff than most other people. But ideally, you will take *at least one* of the nine principles, actively work at mastering it, and later be able to reflect and recognize that you had more success – that you gained greater influence over people and outcomes – after you started applying the principle than you were able to achieve without it. Science tells us that the more you work at improving, the better you will get, no matter where you start from.

MIND TRICKS

This book is not a collection of magic tricks. It will not enable you to read people's minds, perform dope deceptions at parties, or dupe people into paying too much for a second-hand car. Party tricks might excite and impress your friends, but they will not help you build a more successful career.

When you seek to influence people to increase your career success, you cannot afford to sell someone a car that does not work. The key customers, managers, and peers you need to influence cannot be treated as disposable because these players can easily re-emerge at important moments when you need them. As luck would have it, there is often no more certain way to ensure that a particular person will end up being your manager (or the decision-maker for a huge contract) than by totally dissing and burning your bridges with that person.

The ability to influence people and outcomes is a complex skill. Like all complex skills, it can be learned, and your performance will improve the more you practise and work at improving. Further, complex skills of this kind are made up of smaller individual skills that can each be practised and mastered separately. To illustrate, your overall skill level in playing a game of tennis is determined by your ability in many component skills such as serving, hitting volleys, using backhand, and keeping your focus under pressure. In the same way, this book is designed to help you learn individual component skills of exerting influence. You might choose to develop skill in just one of the principles, or you might learn several principles and apply them in combinations. You do not have to read all nine principles to increase your ability to influence people and outcomes, but the more you strive to learn, practise, and apply these principles, the more influence capability you will have at your disposal.

In the short term, appropriate use of these principles increases your likelihood of affecting an outcome, meaning that on average you will exert more influence when you apply the principle than when you do not. In the longer term, your goal should go beyond masterful capability in one or more principles, into increasing the extent to which you are viewed by colleagues and customers as a valuable person with whom they want to work. That outcome is not commensurate with using cool tricks to get someone to pay too much for a dodgy car.

WHAT IS BEHAVIOURAL SCIENCE?

You are a unique and wonderful individual. Of all the members of our species over the previous 250,000 years, no one has ever had the exact same experiences as you. Nonetheless, despite the fact you are unique, every person also has many attitudes, values, and behaviours in common with numerous other people. Behavioural science is a collection of disciplines (including psychology, sociology, behavioural economics and neuroscience) that examine these similarities and differences in what people think and do. For example, if you have ever been exposed to behavioural science in the workplace, this may have been in the form of a diagnostic test (such as a Myers-Briggs assessment) that allows people to compare their relative personality types. Companies can use such diagnostic tools to stimulate better co-operation among their employees by enabling them to recognize and tolerate each other's differences in perspective and attitude.

However, we will not use behavioural science to focus on differences. Instead, we will focus on what is common across most people, most of the time. Although information about each of your unique qualities is important to you – and perhaps to your dating app matches – it is the aspects of behaviour that are common across groups of people that are most actionable from a business perspective. In fact, a great deal of our behaviour occurs in predictable and repeated patterns even though we can't often see that ourselves. Behavioural patterns can be common across most humans in general, or to members of a community, company, or family, or to everyone who has experienced a specific event or situation.

The scientific method involves several stages, generally starting with systematic observation, which is the collection of data in a manner pre-planned to ensure it is methodical and unbiased. Once systematic observation seems to have detected a behavioural pattern, the next stage is systematic testing. This means that the hypotheses about behavioural patterns generated from the observation stage are now tested by taking a neutral situation, introducing the variables or stimuli believed to trigger the behaviour pattern, and then measuring whether or not the predicted outcome does indeed occur as expected. The final stage in the scientific process is to use statistical procedures to calculate the mathematical probability that the outcome observed in the experiment is likely to have been caused by the introduction of that test variable, not by simple random chance. If the statistics indicate that there is a 95 per cent or better probability that the outcome occurred because of the introduction of the test variable, scientists then describe the finding as 'significant'. In other words, we can expect that the tested variable will produce the measured reaction on average, across a population of people represented by those in the study. Note: this does not mean the reaction will occur *every single time*, nor *for every single person*, nor in *every single context* – only that on average, across a large group of people, we can expect to observe the significant result more often than not.

WHY SCIENCE-BASED KNOWLEDGE IS VERY DIFFERENT FROM YOUR OWN OPINION

The scientific process described in the above paragraph is very different from the way in which individuals form beliefs about the world around us. For a start, we cannot afford the time and attention to collect substantial, systematic, and unbiased data about every single thing that happens to us. If we had to do that, it could take us a long time and a lot of pain to learn that bread recently delivered from a toaster can burn our fingers, or that walking in front of a moving car can be dangerous to our health.

Instead, we use shortcuts to screen out a lot of information and focus only on that which our subconscious identifies as important for one reason or other. These shortcuts benefit us so that we can quickly learn not to grab for hot objects or run across the road without looking. However, given that our brains are exposed to millions of data points in any one second, and we can only process a very small proportion of that information, the shortcuts in data selection and processing that keep us alive do not reliably produce an unbiased view of the world. In fact, the beliefs we form using a heavily censored and reduced set of information can also be highly incorrect, even completely ludicrous. They just don't tend to kill us.

To give you one example, let's go back to the dark ages of the 1940s and consider a study of pigeons by B.F. Skinner, one of the early scientists working in behavioural science. Skinner kept pigeons in individual enclosures whereby food was delivered to them for a period of just a few minutes per day. Crucial to the experiment is that the food was not delivered all at once. Instead, small amounts of the total were dispatched at completely random intervals during the feeding time window. The key here is that delivery was random: after the first serving of food occurred, there was literally nothing the pigeons could do to make the next batch arrive any faster. However, that is not how the pigeons behaved. For example, a pigeon that had been turning around at the moment the second batch of food arrived learned to link this turning behaviour to the arrival of more food. As a result, once the first serve was delivered, this individual pigeon started turning in circles as if that would cause the second serve to appear. Another pigeon began bobbing up and down and yet another started nodding its head repetitively. These pigeons developed what Skinner termed 'superstitious behaviour' that we might recognize today in those who believe they can affect an outcome through behaviour that has no impact on that outcome at all. Superstitious behaviour is an example of biased individual data processing that could be identified as false if the scientific process were applied.

If you are thinking to yourself that you are smarter than a pigeon, and therefore you would not fall victim to such a ridiculous set of beliefs, you are wrong. In fact, because your brain is vastly more complex, and is attempting to process such an enormous volume of data at any one moment, the number of demonstrated shortcuts and biases that it exhibits is gigantic. If you search online using terms such as 'cognitive biases' or 'heuristics', you can easily determine that there are literally hundreds if not thousands of ways in which our data-processing units (our brains) are failing to perform a data collection and testing process that is in any way equivalent to the scientific method. As a result, it should come as no surprise that people's typical explanations as to why they do the things they do are often not very good. In fact, behavioural science tells us that these explanations, on average, cannot be trusted at all.

HOW BEHAVIOURAL SCIENCE CAN HELP YOU UNDERSTAND INFLUENCE BETTER

Imagine you have just come home from an evening out during which you ate too much junk food, consumed too much soda or alcohol, and snacked on too many nacho chips. This is not what you had intended at all: in fact, you went to your friend's dinner party determined to eat only healthy food, drink only water and stick to a calorie budget. When reviewing the night, you will likely get angry with yourself and might be tempted to label yourself as a failure. You may believe that if only you had stronger willpower, greater restraint or more discipline, you would not have behaved this way.

So how would your perspective change if you learned from behavioural science that, in fact, when you sit down to eat with people you like, at a table surrounded by tasty food, at the end of the week when you feel like celebrating, there is a 75 per cent chance you will consume twice as much as you would have eaten, had you simply stayed at home? What if science also told you that this is true *even for those who have high willpower*? Armed with this perspective, you might stop seeing yourself as a weak-willed loser and instead recognize that this overeating was simply normal behaviour for the situation, because our choices are strongly affected by social and contextual triggers that influence us without our conscious permission – or even our awareness.

IS THIS GOING TO BE HARD?!

No, it's going to be fun. There is a vast amount of scientific literature on the topic of human behaviour and what influences it, but the purpose of this book is not to turn you into an expert on science – it is to make you more influential in your career. The nine principles included here have been selected specifically because they are the most relevant for professionals seeking to advance their careers by increasing their influence over people and outcomes in the workplace.

Each of the nine principles is covered in one dedicated, stand-alone chapter. Each of these chapters begins with a simply worded overview of the relevant scientific knowledge – that is, what the principle means and how it works to affect us. Next, you will find explanations of how the principle is relevant in a workplace or professional setting. Finally, each chapter contains a range of examples, exercises and advice to enable you to start building your personal influencing skills and identifying opportunities to put that skill into action for your benefit.

The principles themselves are not grouped in terms of scientific phenomenon (as a scientist would do), but instead in terms of categories that will make sense to someone attempting to apply them. In other words, this book is specially designed to help you go beyond mere knowledge so that you can develop real capability.

WHERE TO START

That's up to you. Of course, I recommend starting at the beginning and reading one chapter at a time until you reach the end of this book. However, it is better to do some reading than no reading at all. If you are short on time – or not yet convinced you want to read a whole book! – then choose the topic that interests you most and challenge yourself to complete one chapter. The nine principles are structured into three sets of three as follows:

People-related:
Principle One is *Status*
Principle Two is *Social Imitation*
Principle Three is *Affiliation*

Perception-related:
Principle Four is *Value Framing*
Principle Five is *Effort*
Principle Six is *Reasoning*

Behaviour-related:
Principle Seven is *Inertia*
Principle Eight is *End-Goal Focus*
Principle Nine is *Execution*

Of course, there is a science-based reason for providing you with nine principles: nine is the maximum number of meaningful units of information that our brains can hold in short-term memory. Remembering information also becomes easier when that information is structured into meaningful pieces. As a result, the model provided in this book includes nine principles structured into three units of three principles each.

I hope you enjoy the journey. Good luck and have fun!

Principle One

Status (Where Do You Rank?)

Executive summary

As a social species, we continually evaluate and judge other human beings at both a conscious and subconscious level. When we interact in a professional group such as a team, department, or committee, that evaluation includes ranking other members in terms of their relative status. The status we attribute to others determines the extent to which we are influenced by them. Research indicates that when people receive instructions from someone they perceive as having higher status they do less neural processing than when they act on their own initiative. In other words, they think less before acting. The status we ascribe to others can derive from formal authority, from physical characteristics, or contextual cues. If you want to exert influence in situations where you don't have formal authority, the first step is to understand how human brains conduct status rankings. The next step is to use that knowledge to increase your status relative to other members of the group. In this chapter you will be guided to create a personal preparation plan that will enable you to boost your status and hence your power to influence others.

AUTHORITY AS A POWERFUL DETERMINANT OF STATUS

You may have heard of power dressing for authority – but would you do something you didn't want to do because of the clothing worn by the person who asked you to do it? My postgraduate business school students are generally adamant that they would not, although some admit that a police officer's uniform might carry a degree of influence. What if the clothing in question were a lab coat? If you are unfamiliar with Dr Stanley Milgram's contribution to the field of psychology, you may find the details of these next studies, well, shocking.

Shock tactics

In 1963, a group of adult men volunteered to take part in a study (supposedly of memory) for which Yale University would pay them a nominal fee.[1] When each participant arrived at the laboratory, he was met by the experimenter and another participant. Unbeknownst to the actual volunteer, the experimenter was not a scientist, but merely a male actor wearing a lab coat and glasses. Further, the other 'participant' was in fact a *confederate*, which is a term used to describe sneaky double agents who are actually part of the experimental team while pretending to be normal participants.

The experimenter ensured that the participant was always assigned to the role of the teacher and that the fake participant (aka the confederate) would be doing the learning. The learner was placed in a chair, strapped into the armrests, and then attached to a machine that delivered electric shocks. The teacher was then led to a separate room, where he was asked to sit at the controls to the machine administering the shocks. The fake scientist (aka the actor) carefully explained to the teacher that the range of shocks the machine could deliver ranged from a mild 15 volts only, increasing in 15-volt increments all the way up to 450 volts. A 15-volt shock would produce a slight sensation, a 300-volt shock would cause severe danger and 450 volts would result in certain death. There was a wall between the teacher and the learner, so the participant would not be able to see the learner, although he was able to hear him speak.

The teacher first read aloud a series of word pairs for the learner to memorize. In the next step, the teacher called out a word and the learner had to name its correct pair. The learner gave the correct answer at first, but after a set time interval he made a mistake. At this point, the scientist instructed the teacher to give the learner an electric shock, starting at the low end of the scale – and the learner gave a mild 'Ow!' response.

As the experiment continued, the learner made more and more mistakes. After each mistake, the scientist told the teacher to go one 15-volt step higher in the level of shock administered. Although the teacher could not see his fellow volunteer, he could hear the increasing distress that his actions caused. Whenever the teacher expressed reluctance to continue, the fake scientist used a pre-set series of responses, starting at 'please continue', escalating to 'the experiment requires you to continue', with the final directive being 'you have no choice, you must go on'. In response, these volunteer teachers continued increasing the level of shocks until the learner stopped speaking altogether. The scientist then told the teacher to interpret silence as an incorrect response – and continue with the shocks.

Before the experiment was conducted, the real scientist (Milgram) asked 40 psychiatrists to predict how the teacher would respond to the experiment.[2] The psychiatrists predicted that most volunteers would drop out at 150 volts and fewer than 5 per cent of people would continue to 300 volts. Instead, Milgram found that every single participant continued to the 300-volt shock and 65 per cent of people continued right up to the end. In fact, participants continued administering shocks even when they demonstrated extreme discomfiture over their actions.

If you have never heard of this experiment before, you will be relieved to discover that the learner did not receive any real electric shocks, because the teacher was listening to a recorded voice only. Of course, the fact that no one died is small compensation for the horror of discovering that more than half the participants continued obeying instructions to the point where they believed they had killed a random stranger for the purpose of a memory experiment.

How an actor becomes an authority

For us to understand how Milgram's experiment applies to influence in the workplace, let us first examine how the authority status of the 'scientist' was constructed. First, the participants were ordinary members of the community, who knew they were arriving at a highly prestigious university. Second, they likely perceived the experiment as important because of the prestigious context. Finally, they were told what to do by a person wearing a lab coat and glasses, thus they were perfectly primed to perceive this actor as an authority figure. These contextual and social cues caused them to behave in a way that ran directly against their own moral code.

At this point you may be thinking that those participants were losers, and you would not behave in the same way. You could also be thinking these results aren't relevant today because people were more obedient in the 1960s. At least some readers will be thinking that a *woman* would never do something so deplorable. Sadly, the science suggests you are wrong on all counts.

Milgram's original experiment has been replicated with many different groups of people and the same results were found more than 50 years after the original experiment.[3] Across studies conducted in Jordan, Spain, Australia, South Africa, Poland and the United States, the average proportion of participants who obey to the point of inflicting fatal shocks on strangers remains in the range of 60 to 65 per cent[3, 4]; occurs whether the participants are male or female[5]; and was replicated even when the 'learner' in the experiment was a puppy.[6] It seems the influence exerted by authority is strong across humans in general.

Why would people behave like this? In the introduction to this book, I explained that our overloaded brains take lots of shortcuts because we have huge volumes of data to process at any one time. Research shows that when people receive instructions from someone they recognize as having authority, they do less neural processing than when they act on their own initiative. In 2016, scientists at Duke University used electroencephalography (electrical sensors on the scalp) to measure brain activity during a replication of Milgram's experiments in which participants were instructed to give each other small, but nonetheless painful, electric shocks. Participants reported a relatively low sense of responsibility for the harm they caused, and their brain activity demonstrated they were not processing the consequences of their actions.[7,8] In other words, when they followed instructions from an authority figure, their brains took shortcuts.

As a result of these findings, if you are in a position of formal authority at work, others are predisposed to be influenced by you, provided that a) they are aware of that authority and b) what you are asking them to do is clear (such as the simple act of pressing a button). Thus, from an ethics point of view, your authority endows you with an increased degree of responsibility towards what you ask them to do.

If you don't yet have a high degree of authority in the workplace – or if you wish to influence people over whom you have no formal authority – rest assured that you can create or increase status for yourself within many workplace situations. There are many different components to status and the more you know about them, the better equipped you will be to build your own status and thus your power to influence people and outcomes in the workplace.

YOUR STATUS RANK DETERMINES YOUR INFLUENCE IN THE GROUP

When two or more people get together in either face-to-face or virtual environments, they assess each other in terms of relative status within the group. The process may be conscious but is often unconscious; thus, it occurs whether or not participants are aware it is happening. In behavioural science this practice is described by Status Characteristics Theory[9,10] and you may be surprised to learn that there is a high degree of commonality in terms of the relative rank we inadvertently and silently assign to each other.[11] Further, the factors that influence this perceived status ranking are fairly consistent across cultures.[12,13,14] The outcome of the ranking process has a profound effect on who wields influence in the group and who does not.

When behavioural scientists measure people's interaction during a group activity or discussion, the observed pattern of interaction generally mirrors the group's implicit status assumptions. In other words, the higher the commonly perceived status of a given attendee, the more the group will allow that person to speak. Conversely, the lower the commonly perceived status of a particular person, the less inclined they are to listen to him or her. This pattern is also reciprocal: those perceived as having higher status are also addressed more often and looked at more often by other group members.

The same ideas are rated as more valuable when expressed by someone with higher status and higher-status speakers are less likely to be interrupted.[9] Moreover, the larger the group, the more unequal relative participation in the discussion will become. To illustrate, in a three-person group the individual with the highest status will control about 47 per cent of the group's time, the second, about 30 per cent, and the third, about 23 per cent. As the group gets larger, the highest status individual will continue to control around half of the conversation, with the remaining 50 per cent split between everyone else. Hence, in a group consisting of eight or more people, there will be some members who hardly contribute at all.[10]

As discussed already, a position of formal authority, such as being the boss of all other group members, will endow a participant with relatively high status and thus a significantly greater opportunity to be acknowledged, addressed, and heard compared with other members of the group. Of course, the same individual may not have a comparable degree of influence over family and social activities where the authority of being head of department is not relevant. As we will explore, status can change according to the situation.

Status in the workplace – or any goal-oriented team activity – is determined not only by formal authority but also by physical and contextual factors. The following sections will enable you to better understand the interplay of these factors so that you can design your own action plan for increasing your status in the workplace and thus influencing people and outcomes.

FACTORS AFFECTING STATUS IN THE WORKPLACE

Some factors are purely physical

The first and most apparent source of information used to appraise and rank other people is their physical characteristics. The key physical characteristics that confer status (termed 'diffuse' characteristics by some scientists[15] and 'face-ism' by others[16]) comprise being male rather than female[17,18] being taller rather than below-average height[19], being more attractive, rather than below average in attractiveness[20,21] and being Caucasian rather than anything else.[22]

Age can also affect status. When complete strangers aged 18 to 65 on jury service need to determine a leader for the group discussion, they are four times more likely to appoint a man than a woman, and twice as likely to appoint someone aged over 45 than someone aged 18 to 44 years old.[23] Perhaps you have experienced sitting in a restaurant with a group of diverse people whereupon the waiter brings the bill to the oldest man at the table, assuming that this is the person in charge of the group.

Less is known about how virtual environments affect the perception of physical characteristics and therefore status ranking, although we can infer that the process will be modified. We might predict that height should become relatively less important as a ranking factor, given that online video conferencing renders people to approximately the same height and research suggests that the shoulder-to-hip ratio typically associated with dominance in men does not have a significant effect in virtual environments.[24] Hence, it is possible that virtual environments such as Zoom in which every participant is given equal physical size may reduce status inequality for women. In contrast to physical size, however, it is likely that facial characteristics become more important because we infer leadership ability in both men and women from facial features that include masculinity, femininity and attractiveness[25,26] as well as facial width-to-height ratio.[27]

Fluency in the language of the gathering can also affect status. While not specifically a physical characteristic, fluency is a characteristic that an individual can't change ahead of the meeting and non-native English speakers who are difficult to understand – or non-native speakers of any language in which a meeting is being held – run the risk of being assigned low status. Dr Rebecca Piekkari, from the Aalto School of Business in Finland, studied the pitfalls of a common business language for those who can't speak it fluently. She and her colleagues found that language fluency indeed affects the extent to which a group permits participation and is even used as a tool in power games to limit the voices of non-native speakers.[28,29]

It is important to keep in mind that the members of the group who are failing to listen to you are not necessarily behaving this way because they are judgemental, nasty bullies who are out to get you. Not only is it possible that this entire process has occurred unconsciously, it is also supported by *group consensus*. That taller or older man is not the one putting himself in charge: *everyone* is putting him in charge. In experiments designed to give two participants of different status an opportunity to discuss a topic as equals, lower-status individuals were observed suggesting to higher-status individuals that they take the leadership position in a decision.[30]

These inherent and generally unchangeable physical characteristics are strongly associated with status in ways that are not only consistent across cultures, they exist in similar forms among non-human primates.[16] While in the ape world it may be valuable to associate higher status with the largest and most physically dominant individual, there is no evidence that the ape who is best at aggressively beating opponents into submission will necessarily make the best business decisions. Hence, while it is clearly ludicrous to assume that a taller or more attractive person has a better idea than a shorter or less attractive one, this is nonetheless how groups of people tend to behave.

In summary, if you have ever been at a meeting and felt that no one is listening to you, the depressing news is that you are probably right. On the other hand, if you are a tall, typically masculine Caucasian male, it is possible you have no idea what I am talking about.* For everyone else, the good news is that there are steps you can take to combat 'face-ism' and increase your status among a group at work. The first one is to recognize what kind of advantages or disadvantages you may be confronted with at the outset and then prepare effectively so you can diminish them. It is certainly possible for you to create status for yourself irrespective of your physical characteristics and without having to resort to getting angry, baring your teeth or other human equivalents of beating your chest. It just takes an understanding of contextual cues, some planning, and some practice – much like any complex skill in which you want to improve.

SOME FACTORS ARE CONTEXTUAL AND CAN BE MANIPULATED

The status boosts or decrements determined by contextual factors are more easily manipulated by your personal actions than status conferred by physical factors, particularly if you are well prepared in advance. In other words, you may not walk into a meeting with a job title that indicates authority, or a physical appearance that communicates high status, but you can increase your perceived status if you can demonstrate contextual status factors such as those listed below.

> **Overall level of education**, as well as **prior experience in a specific job role or industry**, can confer relative status. In Feller's (2010) overview of who gets chosen as the jury foreman, people were more likely to be selected if they had a college degree or previous experience on a jury when they were among those who did not attend higher education or had no previous experience.[23]
>
> **Quantified expertise in the topic of discussion** can also elevate your status in a group. For example, if two jury members in the group had a college degree, one in modern languages and

---

*Although you may find you are given the bill at a restaurant

the other in criminology, we might expect the criminologist would be conferred with higher status and more likely to lead the discussion.

In the absence of a degree, a relevant skill or ability can carry implications of competence that will elevate a person's status, particularly if the implied skill set is relevant to the discussion or decision the group is facing. For example, you will be more likely to influence people to accept your solution to a quantitative problem if you have a clear indicator of proficiency in numerical skills, such as a certificate or a good past exam result.

Past achievement in the topic or problem currently being addressed by the group can increase your status. For example, imagine that a new hire is placed in a team working on a logistics problem. They may not have much experience in the given industry, nor any formal qualification in logistics, but he or she would increase in status if able to provide an example of a similar problem they had helped to solve.

Speaking up with confidence. Feller's analysis of jury groups also found that being among the first to speak up was associated with being selected as a group leader and therefore being awarded the highest status among the group.[23] Similarly, in a series of studies – first involving students, then business managers – US researchers found that those who had a narcissistic personality and who therefore behaved in a confident manner were highly likely to be chosen as a leader when put into leaderless groups.[31] In yet another study, researchers found that overconfident men were much more likely to be selected as the leader of a group compared to less confident women who nonetheless had a track record of competence.[32,33] Sadly, but truthfully, humans tend to confuse confidence with capability. If you are less inclined to make your voice heard, it is important to recognize that your personality type in no way renders your ideas less worthwhile. However, to generate status and influence for yourself in a professional group, planning to participate early and confidently will help enormously.

Authoritative, data-based statements can also confer status upon your contribution within a group. To illustrate, imagine a group of people is discussing the best product to stock on retail shelves. One member of the group might argue that the medium-sized product is best because of its superior artwork, while another person argues that the larger product is best because the built-in carry handle makes it more attractive. So long as the argument involves one opinion against another, the person with the higher status will win by group consensus. However, if the lower-ranked person had prepared by accessing the past six months of sales figures and could demonstrate that the larger size product always sells more, then he or she will have dramatically increased the authority of their argument. Moreover, if the same individual continues to prepare such authoritative, data-backed arguments for subsequent meetings, this association with data and hence authority may help to build long-term status within the group.

PLANNING TO INFLUENCE PEOPLE AND OUTCOMES USING PRINCIPLE ONE

In the original paper on status characteristics, Berger and colleagues noted that the mechanism driving the status value of physical characteristics is the often unconscious and biased assumption that they mirror a person's ability to add value to a team effort.[9] In order to counteract these unconscious biases, you must develop skill in identifying contextual status characteristics that you can use to your advantage to increase your status – and thus potential for influence – in any given professional situation.

Preparation for generating status and influence in teams, meetings, and networking events

A personal preparation plan is a good way to begin developing your skill. In each of the following sections, identify how you can apply this understanding to your own background, circumstances and skill set. Your preparation plan can be used not only for team activities, but also for interviews and networking events in which you want to distinguish yourself among your peers. Koski et al. (2015) established that higher-status individuals are not only looked at and listened to more by others, they are also better remembered by the people they have just met.[14]

When making your plan, it is important to be aware that contextual characteristics endow status on an individual under two conditions:

1. They distinguish and elevate you *compared to other members of the group;* and
2. You can display or highlight them in a manner such that *they will be noticed by meeting participants.*

Hence, leveraging contextual status characteristics will require some careful preparation, first in identifying the flexes to use and second in bringing them to people's attention.

1. Prepare in advance to participate

As a behavioural scientist and a university professor, I know that the tendency to speak up and answer a question in a lecture hall has a stronger correlation with personality type than it does with having something useful to say. Unfortunately for people who don't feel inclined to speak up, most managers are not behavioural scientists and are likely to interpret this selective silence as a valid indicator that they don't have anything useful to contribute. Further, once a group starts to leave someone out of the conversation, that tendency will only get stronger the longer it goes on, because interactive patterns of behaviour become reinforced through repetition. Hence, the moment that you have a team meeting or networking event on the horizon, you should make a preparation plan to ensure you have something valuable to contribute.

If the situation is going to be an interview, a seminar or a networking event or a class, you might prepare by writing an insightful question based on work that has been done by a speaker or senior person who will be attending. If worded correctly, such a question can demonstrate to everyone listening that you are well prepared and have knowledge of the topic. If the situation is going to be a team meeting, then brainstorm what objectives the group might be tasked with achieving, work out in advance what input the group will need, and prepare something to take with you. As already noted, being prepared with data-based statements, including facts, figures or a chart can endow you with authority and status. Further, if you have some degree of familiarity Principle Seven (*Inertia*), you'll recognize that most attendees will turn up to the meeting without having prepared anything whatsoever. Once the usual ice-breaker conversations are completed, there will be a pause in activity as people recognize they need to decide on the next step. This pause in group inertia can give you the opportunity to make your input. If you are the one who has prepared a simple, non-controversial three-step process for tackling the issue, this will likely influence what the group does next – and it will add to your status as a key contributor.

2. Don't rely on your job title

When introducing ourselves in a professional setting, we often lead with our job title. We do this because it is easy, not because it is effective in communicating status. In fact, the meaning of a job title in terms of degree of responsibility, seniority and expertise rarely translates well, even between departments in the same large company, let alone between individuals outside of the company. Recall that when introducing yourself, your goal is to establish status relative to those around you. Just as if you were branding a product, look for big impact variables and keep it simple and clear. For example, if you had a junior position – or even a temporary position – at a company with an impressive brand name, you should mention that brand name, rather than give details of the position.

What can you identify about yourself that clearly communicates status? The examples in Table 1.1 may help stimulate your creativity. The key is to identify the right element of your experience and capability and express it appropriately – something that is unlikely to be done simply through a job title.

TABLE 1.1: Some examples of workplace status characteristics that you might use to introduce yourself to a group

Current position	Limited status introduction	Distinctive status introduction
Works in a small IT team	Works in the IT sector	Led the successful rollout of key initiative 'x'
Marketing manager	Works in the soft drinks team	Responsible for a specific recognizable brand or a significant budget
Relationship manager	Works in sales	Landed a major contract with a new client last month
Recently hired into this company	New to the department	Previously worked at Porsche
Just graduated from university	Recent graduate	Has experience in financial modelling

3. What if you don't have relevant work experience?

What should you do if you don't have much relevant work experience? The answer is that we all have something we can use to our advantage – it may just take some effort and creativity to find and express it. Do you have expertise or strong skills in a given area or application? Expertise functions as a form of authority. Examine your strengths against each of the contextual status characteristics described earlier. Do you have a qualification, a certificate, a high exam grade, an example of an achievement or a testimonial from someone who has established status in your chosen topic?

Introducing yourself as 'a student', 'working in the finance sector', 'a business development manager', 'an Egyptian' or any other bland manner neither distinguishes you in any way, nor confers any status. If you have recently been on maternity leave, there is no need to mention that. In fact the data suggests that identifying yourself as a mother has a negative impact on status, while identifying yourself as a father may confer status, but is also potentially risky.[11] In a nutshell, stop thinking of yourself in terms of the labels that most easily come out of your mouth and instead think of labels that are both status-invoking and true.

4. Counteract negative stereotypes

The status ranking effects of our physical features are largely based on cultural stereotypes – and sadly they affect our unconscious judgements, even when we don't consciously believe in those stereotypes.[34] As a result, negative stereotypes that associate a lack of ability in a specific area with a person's physical characteristics can wield a negative effect on that person's status during discussions of the topic, even when they are among open-minded colleagues.

Dr Claude Steele of the University of California, Berkeley, has built an extensive research career examining how people can avoid the effects of negative stereotypes. One of the keys he found is in individuating yourself from the negative label by associating yourself with a contrasting positive label instead.[35] For example, one of his African-American graduate students was disturbed by the fact that strangers on the street crossed the road when he walked towards them coming back from campus at night. He found that he could influence these strangers to feel comfortable walking past him by whistling popular classical music pieces, such as those by the composer, Vivaldi. This activity caused him to be individuated from a negative stereotype (potentially dangerous person) and instead perceived positively (educated person), which was enough to change people's reactions to him. As unpalatable as this topic may be, consider whether or not you might be subject to negative stereotypes about your ability in a given subject, topic or work area. Prepare in advance to counteract those stereotypes. How could you label yourself in a manner that classifies you as a strong performer instead?

5. Choose one or two main flexes for each context

When considering which status cues you wish to highlight in your favour, it is crucial to narrow down the list to your top one or two key strengths for the given situation. Contrary to the popular belief that the more you say the better, people find it difficult to attend to and register large swathes of data. Instead, provide them with one or two very strong, salient points that will stand out and distinguish you.

To help you choose, start by considering what status cues are most relevant to the specific context you are going into, as well as those that carry the most strength for you. Where do you have strong claims to status, or good examples of achievement? Choose the one or two highlights that score highest on both of these factors. For example, if you are going into an environment in which academic achievement is important, an academic qualification will carry more status. Conversely, if you are going into a meeting of sales professionals, ditch the academic lingo in favour of the success you achieved selling sports equipment on eBay, or your year observing what factors cause people to buy expensive jewellery (aka what you learned working in your aunt's shop). You should be thoroughly prepared and practised in using these flexes to introduce yourself so that you can bring them up at any appropriate moment.

6. Look for the right moment so you're not just bragging

Status cues cannot be effective if they are not noticed by the group – but a significant risk exists if you draw attention to your chosen cues in a manner that others perceive as bragging. Further, as we shall explore in Chapter Four, you will wield the most influence in the workplace when you are perceived as both capable *and* likeable. Recent research in this area can help us here and in general the findings can be summarized in two ways.

First, mention the status cue when it seems to be an appropriate moment. For example, if you are meeting a group of people for the first time then you can expect that team members will be asked to introduce themselves, so this is a great time to leverage your chosen status cues. As described by Dr Leslie John and her colleagues at Harvard Business School, sharing personal details when asked to do so – or when others are doing so – helps protect you against being seen as boasting.[36] Similarly, when the group discussion pauses in response to a problem, speaking up to mention that you have experience solving a similar problem will both increase your status and be seen as appropriate. If you have followed this preparation plan, you will have your statements prepared and ready to go, so you can be actively looking for appropriate opportunities.

Second, be careful of the language you use. State the cue simply – for example, 'I worked for Google in Japan' or 'I graduated top of my class in mathematics'. Research shows that using a 'humblebrag' approach – in which a person combines an accomplishment with a complaint (e.g. 'I work so fast that I am bored the rest of the day' or 'I can't believe they wanted me to be spokesperson for the group!') – causes a person to be perceived both as insincere and less competent.[37]

7. Dress for authority and status

Your appearance is another way in which people judge and categorize you, particularly when they come across you for the first time. There is a vast amount of free internet advice on how to dress for work, meetings, and interviews. However, rather than thinking of dressing to look stylish or to look formal, instead think of dressing in line with the status and authority you want to establish. This doesn't mean that you need to wear lots of gold jewellery or that you should come into the meeting wearing the lab coat and glasses of Milgram's experimenter. It means you need to reflect on the strengths you wish to portray and ask 'how would that person dress?' For example, if you want to highlight your membership in a specific society as a status characteristic, wearing a pin from that society adds to the overall picture.

While research on status characteristics tells us that attractive people often achieve higher status in a group, be very careful that you are not dressing to appear sexy. Tighter or more revealing clothing can lead both men and women to rate female candidates as less competent[38] and it is safer to assume this risk exists for men also. Similarly, even small changes in clothing have been found to communicate different status information to observers.[39] Perhaps if you are a well-established authority you can afford to wear what you want, but in the business world if you want to have influence in the workplace, it is safer to dress for authority and status.

8. Don't take established status for granted

After taking action to create status within a certain group, ensure that the characteristics you have established stay visible. While no one wants to hear the same flex about your time at Google in every single meeting, nonetheless you cannot assume that status achieved using situational and contextual cues in one meeting will accompany you to the next. Instead, you may need to find a different way to demonstrate or bring up a status flex until your influential status position is well established in the interactive pattern of the group. Certainly, the best way to build long-term status in a team is to consistently make a visible and valuable contribution, but while that process is underway you may have to reassert your status when, for example, new people join the group. Once you have established yourself as a key contributor, newcomers will be able to tell that you are someone with status from the way that other group members behave towards you.

BETTER THAN YESTERDAY: WHY WE NEED DIVERSE LEADERS

This chapter attempts to provide you with a concise, yet comprehensive understanding of the status beliefs identified by research as influencing most people, most of the time. This is not to endorse the stereotypes and biased reactions on which those status beliefs are based – far from it! While the text here does not address why these specific stereotypes affect our judgements, I have alluded to the fact that we have some of this behaviour in common with other primate groups. Perhaps these shortcuts – such as favouring physically larger, or more confidently charismatic individuals – enabled our besieged tribal ancestors to better survive violent conflict with warring neighbours. However, in today's professional environment we need to leverage a diverse global workforce and harvest the valuable ideas of capable people who come in vastly different shapes and sizes. Hence, we need to work at reducing and removing such stereotypes. The more opportunity people have to experience leaders and successful role models who represent a wide and dissimilar range of physical, social and behavioural characteristics, the less susceptible they will be to mental shortcuts that equate typically primal signals with indicators of merit and value. Hence, the less that physical factors will wield power in workplace discussions and decisions. Further, if you are in a position of authority or leadership in a company, having the humility and self-awareness to work on changing these patterns can result in a wider variety of valuable and potentially innovative ideas for your team or your company.

ILLUSTRATION OF PRINCIPLE ONE (*STATUS*) FIGURE 1

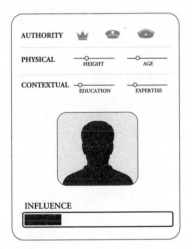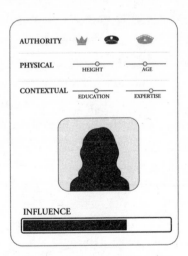

FIGURE 1: Status is determined by a variety of situational, contextual, and physical factors. Your goal is to highlight those that distinguish you and increase your status.

Key takeaways

- Your status relative to others will determine the influence you have within a group, including the extent to which that group allows you to speak, speaks to you, makes eye contact with you, listens to you and values your input.

- The degree of status we attribute to others also determines the extent to which we are influenced *by* them. Studies show that our brains even abdicate substantial aspects of decision-making and responsibility to those whose status we perceive to be sufficiently high.

- A key route to increasing your influence in any situation is to increase the status attributed to you by others in that situation. You can do this by creating a personal preparation plan in which you apply an understanding of contextual status characteristics to your personal circumstances.

- Stop thinking of yourself in terms of the labels that most easily come out of your mouth and instead think of labels you can use that are both status-invoking and true.

- Use the attention you gain from leveraging status characteristics to make a valuable contribution to the group. The earlier you can establish status, and the more consistently you provide valuable inputs, the more you will boost your long-term influencing power within a team.

Principle Two

Social Imitation (The Unseen Influence of Community)

Executive summary

It is common to hear that we choose our own path in life, and we tend to think of ourselves as fully in control of our own behaviour. We see our decisions as a matter of personal values, and our ability to exercise discipline as just a matter of willpower. In stark contrast, behavioural science demonstrates that the community of people around us has a profound, unconscious, and uninvited effect on our behaviour. Our community influences our choices, what goals we set, and how we behave to gain social approval. These influences are not just unconscious – they can even cause us to act in ways that directly contradict our stated values and opinions. As you read about social imitation effects in this chapter, ask yourself if you can think of any specific examples in your workplace, college, or social life. The greater your ability to detect the presence of social imitation influences, the better your opportunity to resist conforming to norms that run against your personal values and might even harm your productivity. Of course, you should also aim to apply your understanding to increase your own influence over people and outcomes in your workplace.

'Monkey see, monkey do' makes a happy monkey

All primates learn through imitating the behaviour of those around them.[1] This is a paradigm that creates common practices among a community and is certainly valuable and adaptive. If you imagine yourself returning from a foraging trip to find your family/tribe/ gorilla troop fleeing from camp, it is probably wise to assume they have good reasons for their behaviour and that you should do the same. It also makes sense that our choices would be influenced by the choices of those who have gone ahead of us – for example, when deciding which restaurant to try, app or download or movie to watch. Social imitation is both a widespread phenomenon and a form of brain processing shortcut that enables your central processing unit to avoid the hard work of having to think for itself. Thus, it should come as no surprise that research shows we modify our behaviour and our choices to align with those of our community. For example, we keep eating for longer when other people around us keep eating[2] and we engage in anti-social behaviour at work if that is how the people around us behave.[3]

Moreover, there is neurological evidence that aligning our choices with those of our peers makes us happy. One study of hungry male and female undergraduate students used magnetic resonance imaging to examine brain activity.[4] Students were asked to rate how much they wanted to eat healthy food (e.g., fruit and vegetables) as well as unhealthy food (e.g., chips and candy). After making their own ratings, they were shown what *they thought* were the average ratings of 200 other undergraduates at the same university. This data had been manipulated so that half of the participants saw data in which their peers preferred healthy foods and half saw data in which their peers preferred unhealthy foods. As we would expect, when students rated these foods again after exposure to the fake peer data, their ratings moved in the direction of what had been most popular with others – whether that was the healthy or the unhealthy choice. However, more than just affecting their subsequent choices, their brain activity revealed how they responded to the information about their peers' choices.

Those who discovered that their original ratings were aligned with those of their (fake) community experienced activity in the region of the brain associated with reward. Further, when students rated the food choices after seeing what their peers had chosen, their neural patterns indicated they were re-valuing that food type. In other words, they were not pretending to like the food liked by their peers, they were genuinely changing their preferences so that what they believed they liked was more in line with the perceived choices of their community. This is just one of the self-inflicted brainwashing techniques through which our community influences our behaviour.

ALL THE WAYS IN WHICH SOCIAL IMITATION AFFECTS US

We imitate choices because it makes decisions easier

Making your own decision is harder than you think. If you've heard of the term 'decision fatigue' you may be aware that our ability to make effective decisions is a limited resource which runs out as we become more tired. Apple's Steve Jobs and Facebook's Mark Zuckerberg had multiple copies of the same clothes because wearing the same thing each day helped reserve decision energy for more important matters. Decision fatigue as a relationship between increased tiredness and reduced objectivity has been measured in the decisions made by orthopaedic surgeons,[5] judges,[6] and consumers,[7] resulting in fewer scheduled operations for patients seen at the end of the week, fewer paroles granted for prisoners seen just before a lunch break and a higher likelihood of impulse purchases after more substantial purchasing decisions that required greater thought.

Mimicking another person's decisions becomes even more likely when you have limited mental energy to expend. In one set of experiments, American students were asked to choose between different brands of Korean tea.[8] Each participant in the experiment was paired with someone whom they thought was a peer but was in fact an actor. As expected, the brand choice of the actor (who chose first) significantly affected the brand choice of the real participant – but this effect became stronger when the participant had also been given a memory task to perform during the experiment. In other words, when their brains were preoccupied with one task, it was easier just to copy someone else on the secondary task.

A follow-up experiment significantly reduced the effect of social mimicry by raising the consequences of the choice: when told they would have to consume the chosen product on the spot, participants did not simply imitate the choice of the person ahead of them. The researchers concluded that people are more likely to mimic other people's choices when they are not thinking too hard – either because they are busy on other things, or because the stakes are relatively low.

We aim to do what is normal and expected

You might think of yourself as a rebel who rejects society's expectations – and this may be true – but it is not true for most people most of the time. The term 'social norm' refers to information we hold (consciously or unconsciously) about the behaviour expected of us in a given situation. For example, when you get into a lift, it is likely you will turn around to face the door and then watch the floor indicator panel (expected behaviour), instead of standing with your back to the door and staring at the people already in the lift (just weird).

When used appropriately, social norms can be powerful tools of influence that are vastly more effective than our logical beliefs about what will influence others to take action. For example, if you wanted to influence guests at your hotel to re-use their towels, you might think it's a good idea to provide reasons why they should do so. It seems logical that providing people with good reasons for an action will influence them to take that action. However – as we shall learn in Chapter Six (Principle Six: *Reasoning*) – providing people with good reasons to do something isn't anywhere near as effective in influencing them as you probably believe. Instead, social normative information provided in the right way at the right time can do the job for you. For example, in a study of hotel guests in Austria and Switzerland, a sign stating '75 per cent of guests who were in this room re-used their towels' led to significantly fewer towels being used compared to the standard message of 'please help us to protect the environment by re-using your towels'.[9] In a study of workplace cafeterias in England and Wales,[10] the basic intervention of putting posters in the cafeteria stating 'most people here choose to eat vegetables with their lunch' led to a significant increase in the purchase of meals containing vegetables – without any need to hold seminars or provide people with good reasons for making that choice.

Information about social norms becomes even more powerful in influencing behaviour when that information carries an implication of social judgement. In a Dutch study of employee behaviour in the workplace, researchers tested different methods for influencing workers to reduce their electricity consumption.[11] They found that the most effective approach was a personalized message from management that included a score, alongside a message of admiration or disappointment, such as '5/10, unfortunate!' or '9/10, great!'. This use of implied social judgement was significantly more effective than offering employees financial incentives for reducing electricity usage, although you can imagine that 'offering incentives' would be near the top of the list if your team were to brainstorm ways to reduce energy consumption at work.

Finally, our underlying beliefs about what is expected and socially condoned in the workplace can lead us to behave in ways that are not in our own best interests and even make us uncomfortable. A survey of 9,000 people in five companies in Paris found that social norms around expected working hours put great pressure on those who had been granted flexible working arrangements to nonetheless arrive at the office 'on time'.[12] The mechanisms that communicated this expectation ranged from employees' personal observations that only people working 'normal hours' were rewarded to sarcastic comments made by managers to flexible workers, such as 'I hope you enjoyed your relaxing morning'. Similarly, a study of young men entering the workforce in Izhevsk, Russia, found they perceived heavy drinking with co-workers to be an unavoidable requirement for being part of the team – and that by adopting this behaviour, they perpetuated the normative belief that bonding through excessive drinking was expected among new recruits.[13]

In summary, your personal observation that everyone at your company answers their emails while on holiday exerts a strong influence over you to do the same, even if your boss tells you directly that you should not feel obligated. In fact, if people in your company wore zebra-print bandanas during work every day, it would be perfectly normal to find yourself out shopping for zebra-print bandanas, no matter how much you hated them. Once there is a shared expectation about how the group behaves, what they wear, what they say, how they act and how they get rewarded, it is pretty difficult to resist joining in.

Social imitation is stronger when we like or feel close to the gang

The power of social norms increases the more we care about being part of the group. A good illustration of this effect comes from a US study that involved 3,700 college students taking online surveys.[14] First, students estimated the average number of drinks they consumed per week. Next, they estimated the average number of drinks consumed per week by each of these four groups: typical college students, students of the same gender, students of the same ethnicity and students from the same sorority or fraternity. Finally, participants were asked to indicate the extent to which they felt close to each of those four group types. Statistical analysis revealed that the more a student identified with a particular group, the closer the relationship between their self-reported drinking and what they considered to be normal for that group. Of course, those participants may have been totally wrong about the number of drinks consumed by each of those four communities, but this finding demonstrates that our brains construct a belief about what we should be doing based on what we think people who are like us are doing.

As you might expect, we are also more likely to conform with the opinions of people whom we like. A Scandinavian study of social media posts determined that it took three times as many likes from a stranger, compared to likes from a friend, to influence a social media user to also like a given post.[15] Further social media research has identified that we are less likely to fact-check a claim made in a social forum, compared to the same claim when we examine it on our own.[16,17] Add to this the increasing extent to which people obtain their news from social media platforms[18,19] and you have a potent means for mass manipulation of opinion.

We feel pressure to conform even when the people around us are wrong – or immoral

The power of social conformity can pressure people into giving the same answer as their teammate, even when they know that answer is wrong. In a famous study (supposedly of vision) conducted by Solomon Asch in 1951, 50 American male undergraduate students were asked to enter a room and take a seat.[20] In every case, the only seat available was the last in a row of seven others, although the participants did not know that this was intentional, nor that the other seven people were confederates. The panel of eight people was shown three lines of different lengths on a screen (A, B and C). Next, they were shown just one of those lines and asked to name which of the previous three it matched. The correct answer was always obvious, but the real participant always gave his answer last.

On the first two runs, all confederates gave the same correct answer, as did the true participant. In the third trial, all seven actors gave the same incorrect answer before the participant spoke. After hearing all seven actors give the same wrong answer, the participant conformed 32 per cent of the time. In comparison, when these same participants did the test on their own, they gave the wrong answer less than 1 per cent of the time. On top of the one-third of people who *knowingly gave the incorrect answer*, some participants declined to give any answer at all and still others gave the correct answer but expressed doubts about their own opinion. Subsequent experiments have replicated the same result in other cultures (e.g., Kuwait),[21] and with female participants instead of men.[22] In other words, hearing everyone else say something that blatantly contradicts the evidence right in front of our faces can have a substantial impact on our own answers.

While you may think it is not such a big deal to give an incorrect answer about the length of a random line, take a moment to consider that this was a situation in which 1) there was an actual correct answer and 2) that correct answer was obvious. Many situations in which we find ourselves have no such clearly correct answer and so this drive to conform is effectively reducing the range and creativity of ideas expressed in a group. Perhaps more troubling are the results from recent studies confirming a similar drive towards group conformity, even when the group is redefining what is morally and socially acceptable. German and Dutch researchers conducted experiments in which Dutch men and women were asked to rate the extent to which they agreed with the morality and decency of various acts, such as eating parts of your dog after it was hit by a car.[23] They found that when seated among three actors, the participants modified their ratings of what was moral and decent to be in line with the much more extreme (but fake) scores *they thought* had been given by the total strangers sitting next to them.

We use social imitation to evaluate our own performance

First described by Festinger way back in 1954, Social Comparison Theory states that we have a drive to evaluate our own performance by comparing ourselves to people around us.[24] You can probably recognize many examples from your own experience. Perhaps you felt pleased with your test grades, only to take an ego blow when you discovered that your friends did better. Maybe you were too scared to jump off a ledge into the sea, but when your little brother did it, you felt compelled to prove you could do it too. Comparing ourselves to those around us – and then feeling proud, depressed, or motivated to improve – is an everyday experience. Our definitions of good vs bad, attractive vs unattractive, high achievement vs low achievement are all heavily influenced by the subset of people with whom we choose – or are forced – to make a comparison. Social comparisons are often labelled by behavioural scientists as 'downwards' (made with people worse off than us) and 'upwards' (made with those doing better than us). While downwards comparisons generally make us feel good about ourselves, upwards comparisons may be either motivational or leave us feeling flat.

The key to a person feeling motivated by social comparison is to ensure the gap between that person's current performance and the performance of those ahead of them is not very big. Researchers from Singapore and Belgium ran a series of experiments designed to represent some of the different ways in which people compare their performance to that of online communities.[25] These activities included online gaming, losing weight, daily step counts and reducing your carbon footprint. They found that when people are in the process of working towards a target, they are motivated by others who are just ahead of them, rather than those who have already completed the journey. Similarly, in a study of tens of thousands of people enrolled in Massive Open Online Courses (MOOC), Dutch researchers found that providing weekly feedback to participants on how their engagement level compared with others in that same week significantly increased course participation and eventually, course completion rates.[26] Their choice of using weekly (instead of monthly or quarterly) feedback ensured that the gap between the influence target and those ahead of them was relatively small and therefore motivating.

One important aspect of our tendency to use other people's performance to evaluate ourselves is that this carries over into the goals we set. Whether you are disappointed because you completed only one pull-up when everyone else did 10, or excited because you sold three products when no one else sold any, it might be worth pausing for a moment and asking, 'If I did not know how others performed, what would my goal be?' In other words, are the expectations of the people around you helping you, or limiting your goals?

Social imitation influences us even when we don't believe it does
Even as you read this, you might still be tempted to think of yourself as an individual who does not give in to peer pressure. Certainly, the existence of these effects does not mean that everyone behaves the same way all the time. It means that what we say and do is invisibly

shaped by our social environment, usually without our noticing at all. Social imitation effects are not only subtle and unconscious, they can even directly contradict our conscious beliefs. In fact, the messages that people consciously rate as being most *unlikely* to influence their behaviour can be those that are actually the most effective at influencing them into action.[27] Similarly, pedestrians were found to be eight times more likely to donate to a street performer when they witnessed another person donate, even though the explanations they gave for the reason they donated were based on personal reasons, such as liking the music, or feeling sorry for the performer.[28] As will become a common theme throughout this book, our conscious explanation of what drives us can't be trusted, because our behaviour often tells a different story.

IDENTIFYING SOCIAL IMITATION INFLUENCES IN YOUR PROFESSIONAL ENVIRONMENT

Some exercises to get you started

We have covered a lot of scientific understanding in this chapter because the influencing factors involved in social imitation are both numerous and profound. The first step in developing your skill in applying Principle Two in your workplace is to develop your ability to recognize social imitation influence factors when they occur. This section contains two exercises to get you started.

Exercise One: Identifying social imitation in common workplace situations

Table 2.1 provides examples of the types of social imitation influences that are common in workplace situations. For Exercise One, review this table and make notes on any similar examples that you have personally witnessed. This exercise helps build awareness.

Exercise Two: Making your own workplace observations (like a primatologist)

You may have heard of Dr Jane Goodall and her work with wild chimpanzees in Gombe Stream National Park, Tanzania.

TABLE 2.1: Some examples of social imitation factors that are common in the workplace

Event	Social imitation factor at play	Potential for influencing
A colleague has just been publicly reprimanded by the team's manager for telling a racist or distasteful joke	This action communicates a social norm about the expected behaviour in team meetings	The rest of the team becomes more likely to self-censor any comment that might be interpreted the same way
A poster on the wall of the bathroom reminds you that you are expected to wash your hands	Social referent information is encountered in the appropriate situation at the appropriate time	Increased likelihood of people washing their hands
An analysis shared companywide reveals that all top performers at your level share a characteristic (e.g. respond to emails within one day)	Information is shared about a group that it is desirable to be a member of	Increased likelihood of employees adopting that behaviour
You don't know how to proceed with a project. You learn that most employees in your situation used a particular template	It is difficult to work out what to do – until you discover what others did	You look for the same template and use it as a basis, even if you modify it
Your work group is trying to decide between Option A or Option B. Someone discovers that every other department chose Option B.	Your group will feel pressure to do the same. That pressure will increase if decision-makers are tired after a long meeting and decision fatigue sets in.	Increased likelihood the group chooses Option B.

Dr Goodall was the first scientist to systematically observe and document the behaviour of free-living chimpanzees, recording their habits and patterns in different situations at different times of the day.[29] During Exercise Two, it may help to imagine that you are Dr Goodall, that your work environment is a national park and that your colleagues are a hitherto unstudied population of primates. Your challenge is to identify the social norm expectations and behavioural patterns in your work environment, thus converting this knowledge from being unconscious and implicit to being conscious and examinable. Attempt to document common behaviour patterns observed in your peers, your managers, and the most senior managers visible to you. The more specifically you can define the social norms and unconscious expectations of your work environment, the better placed you will be to recognize how they influence you and others around you.

Table 2.2 provides a template that can help you to structure these observations. Set aside 15 minutes to record your first impressions and then review your answers on a regular basis. If you have a trusted co-worker, you might ask him or her to do this also so you can compare your answers. If you are new to the company, it can be helpful to ask these questions to someone trustworthy who has more experience to get additional perspective. This exercise enables you to deepen your understanding of social imitation factors in your own professional life.

PLANNING TO INFLUENCE PEOPLE AND OUTCOMES USING PRINCIPLE TWO

There are multiple factors outlined in the preceding sections that you can apply to influence people and outcomes in the workplace. Appropriate use of these factors requires preparation, particularly in the identification of the social information you need. Ideally, repeated practice in a low-stakes environment will help you build up your skill level before you face an important situation. You can't just whip out a top-end game of tennis at the very moment you

TABLE 2.2: Template for analyzing common behaviours in your work environment

Examples of behavioural patterns you might observe frequently across your team or department members	Your observations	Is this pattern beneficial or counterproductive?
Daily Patterns What are the most common daily patterns you observe among your team members? What behavioural patterns have you observed among the senior managers most visible to you? Are there common patterns in when people are available or unavailable? Does this differ for different roles or levels of seniority?		
Expectations of Reward and Punishment What are the behaviours or characteristics that you perceive as being rewarded in your company? What are the behaviours or characteristics that you perceive as being punished or frowned upon in your company? How would you describe the people who get promoted? Compare this to those who don't get promoted.		
Appearance and Habits How do people dress in your team? Does this differ between groups or levels of seniority? Are there common forms of expression or terminology used by your manager and your team? Are people generally respectful or rude? How does this differ across groups? Do they criticize or engage in negative gossip or not?		

have to beat a strong competitor, you must develop that level of skill over time.

Influencing a specific decision-maker

To influence a decision-maker, one of the best places to start is the use of social referent data. The ideal situation occurs when you have information to demonstrate that many people similar to the decision-maker chose the option that you recommend. This will take some investigation from your side. There are two questions to consider:

1. What group labels might the decision-maker recognize as applying to him or herself? How would they label themselves?
2. Can you obtain information about the decisions that have been made on this same topic by people with whom the decision-maker would feel connected?

To illustrate, perhaps you want to influence your manager to permit you to take annual leave at a time that overlaps with another team member. What information can you obtain about the holiday patterns of employees in other teams in your company to convince them that it is a good idea? If you could show your manager that the best-performing teams of comparable size in your company have had up to three teams on holiday at the same time without a drop in productivity, you may influence him or her to be more favourable to your suggestion. If you want the panel to choose Option B from a set of several options, present information showing that Option B is the usual preferred choice among comparable groups. In general, collecting information about 'what other people do' (referent groups the target person considers important) and presenting it at the right moment can be useful in influencing others to adopt similar approaches. Of course, no influence approach is guaranteed to get you the outcome you want, but this recipe will increase your influencing power.

Influencing a potential client or customer

As we saw in the study on choice of Korean tea brands,[8] the brand choice of purchasers can be influenced by witnessing what others ahead of them choose. In the same way, you may be able to influence potential clients to approach you or reach out to you if they see comparable others doing the same. For example, if you had an opportunity to present your company's services to a forum of potential customers, it would be extremely valuable to arrange for a big-name former client to endorse you during that presentation. Make sure the audience is aware of the identity of the person endorsing you. Similarly, you could use social referent data to present your company or your services as the normal choice of comparable referent groups. Can you collect data to show that the best-performing companies in this sector hire an external provider like yourself to deliver this service? Even better if the data indicate that the best companies hire you!

Be careful with exactly what information you show. As a budget holder at Procter & Gamble, I was often approached by external research companies claiming to work for competitors such as Unilever. Instead of persuading me to want to work with them, this information made me concerned that any results we obtained would not be kept confidential (although I did not voice those objections to them). On the other hand, if those same companies had been able to show me that 75 per cent of top performing but *non-competing* consumer goods companies had been very happy with their services, this would have made them look like a valuable and simple choice.

If you can't provide data showing that your company or your service is a frequent choice among people similar to the target person, you can still position your company or your service as a normative choice if you can demonstrate that you are endorsed by someone they like. Can you obtain a reference – or a glowing testimonial – from a friend or co-worker of the influence target, or perhaps from someone whom the influence target admires? Recall we experience more pressure to conform with the opinions of those we like than with those of strangers.

Influencing outcomes in meetings

If you are going to attend a meeting at which many decisions will be made, and you want to influence those decisions, there are several preparation steps to consider:

1. **Choose your battles carefully**. As discussed, it is easier to use social imitation factors to influence decisions that are perceived as less important compared to those seen as more important because more important decisions induce more detailed examination. It might be a better use of your time to influence a small decision and have it go your way than to attempt to sway a major decision and lose (see also Principle Eight: *End-Goal Focus*).

2. **Consider the existing degree of certainty and passion about the topic**. It is easier to influence decisions using social normative information when there is more uncertainty about the right way forward. If there is both uncertainty and relatively low passion, data that infers what is 'normal' or 'what most people do' becomes even more powerful in influencing the choices made.

3. **Consider the order in which decisions will be made**. Meeting attendees typically expend a lot of discussion on the topics that occur early in the agenda and will often be suffering from decision fatigue later in the meeting. This will render them more susceptible to social imitation choices. Choosing what other people have done, or what most groups do, is an easy way to decide when you are tired.

In summary, if the decision you want to influence is: a) of medium-to-low importance by the group in comparison to other decisions or b) not one on which people have strong opinions or a clear approach, or c) it is addressed halfway through the meeting or later, you are in a good position to influence the decision if you prepare relevant normative data about what most people do in this situation. As an extra step, seek out the support of two or more allies in advance of the meeting such that they will enthusiastically support your suggestion out loud when you bring it up. The additional social pressure on top of the factors mentioned above will increase your influencing power.

STRATEGIES FOR AVOIDING COUNTERPRODUCTIVE OR NEGATIVE SOCIAL IMITATION INFLUENCES AT WORK

The template presented in Table 2.2 includes a prompt to consider whether these common behaviours are beneficial or counterproductive. For example, if you are more productive when working remotely, then you might classify having to go to the office every day as counterproductive. Similarly, it may be commonplace for your peers to engage in negative gossip during lunchtime, although that behaviour could be contrary to both your productivity and the person you want to be. If you want to overcome the influences drawing you in the direction of imitation, you are going to need a strategy.

Substitution: Choose a salient badge of group membership to replace the practice you want to avoid

The practices that are common to the group function as a signal of group membership. The more important that membership is to you, the stronger the pressure to mimic those practices. One strategy to lessen the impact of your withdrawal from an aspect of the group's cultural behaviour is to identify an alternative badge of group membership and ensure it is highly visible.

Example – You are a European person working in a Japanese company where the unspoken norm is to work late. Though not mandatory, it demonstrates loyalty to the company. You achieve great output during the day and want to stop work at 6 p.m. to spend time with family and friends. You are already learning Japanese. To demonstrate that you are loyal to the team in a highly visible manner you regularly set aside time right before you leave to practise Japanese aloud in the office with colleagues.

Whatever the practice from which you wish to excuse yourself, the substitute strategy must be strong, visible, and frequently occurring. If people cannot be reminded of it on a daily basis, it cannot substitute for a highly visible daily practice.

Challenge a common practice through data preparation and communication

Recall that some counterproductive practices are in place simply because they represent people's unconscious expectations rather than conscious thought. In the study we reviewed of the social forces causing thousands of French executives with flexitime benefits to conform to standard working hours, management interpreted long working days as an indication of job commitment, putting pressure on employees to conform to expectations. Nonetheless, the research includes verbatim examples of managers who recognized – once they took the time to think about it – that it was unfair to judge flexitime employees based on working hours.[12] Similarly, the researchers who found that people were less likely to fact-check claims made in a social forum were able to overcome that effect by reminding participants of the importance of fact-checking right before the exercise.[16] We know that knee-jerk behaviour patterns can be overcome through interventions that create conscious attention to the desired behaviour.

Avoid conformity in meetings (but pick your battles)

One of the business benefits of teamwork should be that assigning a variety of team members to a project will result in a rich diversity of perspectives. Yet, during this chapter we have learned that it can be difficult to voice an opinion that goes against the majority perspective already expressed. Recalling what we covered in Chapter One (Principle One: *Status*) it can be even more difficult if that majority opinion was contributed by team members of high status.

If you have a contribution to make that significantly differs from the group's consensus, here are some factors to consider before deciding what to do:

- **One dissenting voice makes a difference**. In replications of the original experiment by Asch, results identified that it takes three people giving the same answer to create the conformity effect.[30] However, the tendency to conform drops significantly if even one person expresses dissent. Hence, your willingness to express a different idea in your team meeting could be the stimulus required to encourage others to speak up.
- **Nonetheless, choose carefully when and how often you speak up.** Studies have found that employees who form a habit of challenging or expressing doubts about the majority opinion run the risk of being perceived as less loyal by their managers compared to employees who routinely voice support for ideas.[31] In other words, do not form a routine of always being the critical voice. If you want to avoid establishing a reputation as the critical voice, suggest that the team could rotate the role of 'devil's advocate' to strengthen their ideas.

BETTER THAN YESTERDAY: LEADERS SHOULD AIM TO RAISE BEHAVIOURAL STANDARDS

The ethical behaviour of senior management is an extremely potent source of information to employees about what kind of behaviour is accepted or punished because the actions of those in leadership indicate powerful social norms. When workers see (or believe) that people above them fail to punish questionable acts, or worse, engage in those questionable acts themselves, it sends a powerful signal that adopting the same behaviour will not have serious consequences. Indeed, the single best predictor of sexual harassment in the workplace is simply the perception that the organization does not punish it.[32, 33, 34]

Senior managers are ultimately responsible for the overall behavioural standards of employees, in large part because their behaviour conveys social norms. The literature on social norms is replete with many examples in which a concerted effort from senior figures, using the tools described here, has led to decreases in bullying, harassment, financial misconduct and fraud, as well as increases in safety-related behaviour and improvements in working conditions. As you increase in leadership status you must consciously decide what kind of workplace you will play a role in creating: with great power comes great responsibility!

ILLUSTRATION OF PRINCIPLE TWO
(*SOCIAL IMITATION*) FIGURE 2

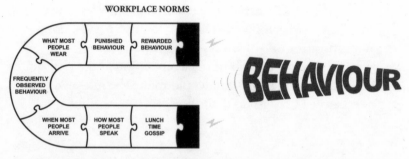

FIGURE 2: We are heavily influenced by both our conscious and subconscious understanding of the behaviour that is expected or normal in a situation.

Key takeaways

- You are far more influenced by what you see other people do, and what you understand to be normal or expected behaviour, than your conscious mind recognizes.

- You are likely to mimic the choices and behaviours that you observe frequently in members of your community – for example, your company or workplace, as well as the frequently observed behaviours of your friends or other social groups.

- The influencing power of social mimicking factors increases when 1) the referent group is important to you; 2) there is more uncertainty about what to do; 3) the decision is relatively low-stakes and will therefore involve less conscious scrutiny and 4) you are suffering from decision-fatigue.

- You can use your knowledge from this chapter both to influence outcomes and decisions, and to help you avoid conformity with negative behaviours, but it will take planning and preparation (ideally plenty of practice too).

Principle Three

Affiliation (Better to Be a Lovable Fool or a Competent Jerk?)

Executive summary

Although it might seem obvious that we are influenced more by people we like than those we dislike, you may not realize the full extent to which one person's sense of affiliation for another can influence their perceptions and decision-making. The simple act of highlighting a degree of similarity between yourself and other people may be all that is required to increase your influence with them. Decision-makers might feel affiliation towards someone who graduated from the same school, who shares the same opinion, who looks like them, who knows the same people or even someone who has the same first name. Being able to create a sense of affiliation between yourself and other people can help to tip decisions in your favour during an interview, a client meeting, a performance review or when you are seeking help, advice, and resources. In this chapter you will discover ways to create a wide range of positive relationships that increase your influence at work without having to be everyone's best friend. Principle Three is one of the easiest principles to learn and to apply – perhaps the hardest part is just remembering to take the time to use it.

WHO DO YOU CHOOSE: A JERK OR A FOOL?

It is the end of the working day and starting to get late. You urgently need help completing an important task. The stars of the department signed off long ago, but two other people are available. One is a person you like, but who is below average in competence. Let's call this person a lovable fool. The other is a person you dislike, but who is above average in competence – in other words, a competent jerk. Which one do you choose?

When Casciaro and Lobo asked this question of employees in three different types of company, they found that people overwhelmingly said they would choose the competent jerk over the lovable fool.[1,2] Similarly, when I pose this question to corporate audiences and in university classrooms, most participants give that same answer. Yet, as you will find repeated in this text, people are not particularly good at predicting what they *would* do in a hypothetical or imaginary situation because when we imagine our future behaviour, we overemphasize our rationality and undercount the influence of emotion in the situation.

When these researchers compared what people *actually did* with what they *said they would do*, they found that employees were significantly more likely to approach the better-liked, less competent colleague (aka the 'lovable fool') instead of the disliked but competent person (the 'competent jerk'). A very similar result was found by researchers at the National University of Singapore, who gave students descriptions of potential work partners that had been manipulated to model either high or low competence and high or low likeability (without specifically using these labels).[3] Their results confirmed that the effect of likeability was nearly twice as high as the effect of competence in determining who people chose as a partner.

It seems that the value of a co-worker's competence and capability is mediated by the extent to which people want to collaborate with him or her. In other words, a competent jerk's competence may even be irrelevant if the person is *too much* of a jerk.

SHOULD A COMPANY CARE WHETHER OR NOT YOU LIKE YOUR WORK PARTNERS?

It seems that people who work with people they like produce better-quality work than employees who are merely lumped together regardless of preferences. In an innovative study of suppliers registered on the microtasking platform *CrowdFlower*, researchers gave participants an opportunity to 'speed date' potential teammates by working with a randomly selected teammate in a dedicated chat room to create a simple advertising slogan.[4] Following the interaction, participants were transitioned to an evaluation page where they entered compatibility ratings for their partner. This procedure was repeated three times with three different partners. Co-workers were then sorted into three pairing types: 1) **Preferred dates**, determined by an algorithm that maximized mutual compatibility ratings of the pair; 2) **Random dates**, pairs of people who had worked together on the first task created at random irrespective of compatibility ratings and 3) **Random non-dates**, i.e. pairs of people with no experience of working together, chosen at random. The three types of team were then asked to create a slogan for a fictitious non-profit organization. The quality of work produced by these pairs was independently evaluated in terms of originality and likelihood of being selected by a customer and the results showed that teams of 'preferred dates' significantly outperformed both of the other two team types (with no significant difference between the work of the other two teams).

In summary, employees are influenced by co-workers they like in several ways: they are more likely to seek them out, more likely to choose them as partners and more likely to do their best work while working with them. However, this is just scratching the surface in terms of the ways in which our affiliation to other people influences our decisions and behaviour.

WHAT DETERMINES WHO WE LIKE?

Perhaps you think you *don't like* people – and you could be an outlier – but most of us need social affiliations. After all, mammal species are generally social species. If you have ever heard of Maslow's Hierarchy of Needs you may know that Maslow's influential Theory of Human Motivation ranks our need for a sense of social belonging and affiliation with others as our most important need as soon as we have secured food, water and safety.[5] Although your personality type influences the form and frequency with which you seek out social interactions, nonetheless the desire to be part of a group is a basic and universal driver of people in all societies.[6] So then, what determines our feelings of affiliation towards others?

We like people whom we perceive as similar to us in prominent ways

In a French study from the University of Lille du Nord, students who thought they were taking part in a study of communication were asked to recount a recent event while wearing electrodes stuck to their head (supposedly to measure emotion).[7] In the next step, participants were asked to wait in another room until the second part of the experiment could begin – and they were given a choice about where they could wait: 1) in a room with another student, or 2) in a room on their own. If participants were told the other student had also taken part in the experiment (similarity of experience), or that the other student had experienced an emotional reaction like their own (similarity of feeling), then they chose to wait with the other student. When told the other person was just a student waiting for an appointment with a professor, they were more likely to choose waiting on their own. In other words, students who had just undergone the fairly weird experience of taking part in an experiment with electrodes stuck to their heads felt affiliation towards those who had just had the same weird experience, but not towards another student also enrolled at the same university.

This experiment helps to highlight that the parameters we use to determine whether or not someone is like us change from one context to another, depending on what factors are salient at the time. For example, a fellow Australian who is not at all like me because he or she supports the rival team at a sports match might suddenly become the only person like me when we are waiting in a faraway airport lounge and no one else speaks English.

A branch of social psychology termed Social Identity Theory provides more perspective. According to Polish psychologist Henri Tajfel, one of the reasons that we have a strong need to affiliate with others is that we define the social groupings in which we belong to create a sense of personal identity.[8] As a result, we categorize and label the people around us in order to define who we belong with – and who we do not. Once we perceive certain people as being in the same classification or grouping as ourselves, we tend to favour them. Behavioural scientists describe this with the term 'in-group versus out-group' bias. It is a well-established phenomenon that the mere act of dividing people into groups is enough to stimulate in-group favouritism, as well as out-group discrimination.[9] In fact, the perception that another person is a member of your in-group has been shown to have profound effects on judgement, including a biased perception of their actions, words, facial expressions, motives and experience of pain.[10, 11]

Our criterion for distinguishing who is 'in' and who is 'out' does not need to be meaningful, it just needs to be prominent at the time. Groups that have been formed on the basis of practically meaningless criteria, such as school children's preference for one painting over another, or the shirt colour that a sports team chooses for just one game, can almost immediately result in more favourable behaviour towards people perceived as belonging – and more punitive behaviour towards those who do not.[12,13] A study of thousands of populist voters in Switzerland, France, Germany and the UK found the movement defines itself as those who oppose ideas expressed in mainstream media.[14] This specific criterion for defining who is in and who is out enables prominent figures in the movement to state whatever suits their best interests without the need for any supporting evidence – and to exhibit hostility towards those who disagree. Further, recent research has suggested that humans can make in-group vs out-group distinctions from as early as 17 months of age.[15]

The key thing to remember is that decision-makers *are going to classify you* in ways that can make you seem like them or not like them – and you will have more influence if you are classified as 'in-group' when the decision is made.

We like people who like us first

An even more powerful determinant of who we like is whether or not other people like us first. In a University of Texas study, researchers asked male undergraduates to meet in pairs for a facilitated discussion. After the discussion, participants were asked to write feedback about their partner, and when both had finished, the feedback was shared. Unbeknownst to participants, one member of each pair was an actor and his feedback was scripted so that it included a perception of their similarity in attitude (high vs low) and the extent to which he liked his partner ('a profound and interesting person' vs 'a shallow and uninteresting person'). In the final step, participants completed a confidential, unshared survey indicating how much they would enjoy working with that partner again and how much they liked him. The results showed that knowing their partner liked them significantly increased the extent to which participants rated that partner as someone they liked and wanted to work with again – more so than whether or not they had similar attitudes.[16]

We like people who praise us and show they care about us

Hearing praise makes us feel good and helps us to like a person. In fact, the simple act of seeing a positive adjective such as 'trustworthy' paired with a picture of one's own face lights up the same reward-related area of our brains associated with receiving monetary rewards.[17] The well-established phenomenon of classical conditioning* tells us that if a particular person appears frequently under conditions that make us feel happy, then it is only a matter

---

* Also called Pavlovian conditioning

of time before the mere sight of that person is enough to induce the same happy feelings: hence a person who repeatedly makes us feel good should become someone we like.

However, what is remarkable about scientific studies of the effects of praise and compliments is the evidence of just how easily and quickly we can be influenced to like someone if they say the right things. A meta-analysis of 69 studies examining the effects of ingratiation tactics such as praise found that even very simple interactions – for example, when people receive compliments about their opinions or intelligence from someone they just met – are enough to significantly increase liking for that person.[18] The effect is even more pronounced when it occurs in a lateral or downward direction within an organization compared to an upward direction (in simple terms, praise for a peer or direct report has a stronger effect on liking than praise for a supervisor).

It is important to exercise care in the use of praise and compliments. People are not idiots. Continual, clumsy overuse of generic praise can readily become obvious, appearing insincere and even creepy, which will have a negative effect on the recipient.[18] Further, research has indicated that acts intended to be kind, such as giving compliments, may not be well received by some people who are low in trust.[19] As such, compliments should be used thoughtfully and genuinely, focused on aspects of a person's performance, ideas or approach that you can genuinely admire. An alternative approach to using compliments is the approach of 'showing care', through acts such as asking about a person's day (and listening to the reply!) or remembering a significant event in their lives and asking about it when appropriate. Showing care is another means to build trust and a positive relationship with co-workers.[19]

As is the case throughout this book, when considering how to apply this scientific understanding to influencing people and outcomes in your workplace, focus on appropriate and ethical applications of your knowledge. Your goal is to build long-term influence in the workplace, not to dupe people or pull fast tricks because deceptions have a high risk of being noticed and eventually harming your affiliations and relationships.

How liking and affiliation affect outcomes in the workplace

As you have seen in the examples covered, we are influenced by people we like in many ways – from being more likely to want to work with them to being more likely to want to share a waiting room with them. If you stay alert for these types of influences in your daily life you will become more adept at noticing their operation around you, and that improved understanding can help you increase your capability to apply your knowledge.

Our evaluations of employees and job candidates are influenced by affiliations

Based on our discussion of the in-group effect, you will recognize that the degree of similarity a hiring manager perceives between themselves and a job candidate will subconsciously affect how that candidate is evaluated. In fact, in-group biases in hiring decisions are so commonplace that the term 'affinity bias' is often used to describe discriminatory processes in candidate evaluation.[20] An Australian study of human–robot interaction even showed that the physical appearance of an avatar was enough to induce an affinity bias that affected how a resume was rated![21] Studies have shown that in-group bias can lead people to make more positive attributions of the reasons an applicant was laid off from a previous job[22] and that in-group bias affects people's evaluation of a candidate even when they consciously state they are aligned with a fair and egalitarian approach.[23] Given the prevalence of these effects it is likely that you have experienced something similar yourself. For example, you may have found yourself feeling more positive about one of your colleagues once you discover they attended the same school as you. You may also find yourself viewing employees of a competitive company as 'the enemy' even though you originally applied to work at that other company also.

In Chapter Two (Principle Two: *Social Imitation*) we learned that we are less likely to fact-check the claims made by people with whom we feel affiliated. I have a painful experience of falling victim to this influence. Several years ago, a manager from an unrelated department told me that his employee would be the perfect candidate to fill a vacant position on my team. He was about the same level of seniority as me and leading a complementary department, which influenced me to perceive him as similar to me. Eight months later, it was clear that the candidate was a low-performing employee whose manager had found it easier to try to move the person into my team than face the stress of managing a redundancy himself.* I hope that the lesson learned from that experience helps me to avoid making the same mistake in the future. The combined influences of the opinion of someone who seems to be a member of our group, together with a reduced tendency to fact-check that person's opinion, are powerful influences on our decisions.

We are more likely to agree to requests from people we like (and who have similar names)

In a series of studies conducted on yet more American undergraduate students, participants were first asked to read a scenario about a person whose name had been either 1) formulated to be very similar to their own, 2) formulated to be familiar to them (the most statistically common names of the time) or 3) had been generated at random. For example, if a participant from the first group was named Cynthia Johnston, she might read about a character called Cindy Johanson. The scenarios people read were identical except for the names of the characters. Participants were asked to rate how much they liked

---

*Principle Five (*Effort*) explains that people are most likely to do whatever is easiest for them

the character in the story. Results showed that both male and female participants who read about a character with a name very similar to their own rated that person as more likeable – and importantly they showed a greater willingness to do that person a favour.[24] In a follow-up test of this finding, the same research team asked a sample of college professors to complete a questionnaire that they received, together with a cover letter from a person supposedly requesting their help. Again, the names on the cover letters were manipulated according to the conditions of the original studies. As predicted, participants returned completed questionnaires at a significantly higher rate when the name on the cover letter was similar to their own.[24] In summary, you are significantly more likely to do a favour for someone, or comply with their request, if you have a reason to like them, even if that reason is just that they have a similar-sounding name.

We give higher performance ratings to people we like or who are likeable

We give more favourable evaluations to people we like on a variety of different performance parameters. The meta-analysis of 69 independent studies of ingratiation techniques mentioned earlier in this chapter[18] found an overall significant effect of an evaluator's liking of a person on how they rated that person's performance – for example, during a debate or discussion. In another study, European, American, and Indian men and women were asked to work in pairs for an exercise that involved negotiating the price of three products. The higher the ratings they gave their partners on likeability, the higher they also rated them on their collaboration skills.[25]

Researchers also found that people who were told a particular doctor was pleasant and likeable before they watched them in a video recording gave higher performance evaluations to that doctor's advice than participants who saw the exact same video clip but had been told in advance that the doctor was unpleasant and unlikeable.[26] In a similar study, college students were asked to read the text of a professor's speech in which that professor advises students to pursue a broad general education instead of a more specialized path. When told that the professor liked the students being addressed, participants gave higher ratings to the professor's advice than those who read the exact same text but were told instead that the professor did not actually like the students in the audience.[27] In other words, the exact same performance is given a higher evaluation when the evaluator believes the performer is likeable than when the evaluator believes the person is unpleasant or unlikeable.

PLANNING TO INFLUENCE PEOPLE AND OUTCOMES USING PRINCIPLE THREE

Evidently, a perceived affiliation between you and a person deciding to hire or promote you can have a profound impact on outcomes in your workplace. Although many organizations today have generated initiatives aimed at reducing implicit bias in such decisions (e.g.[28]) – as they should – nonetheless, we have seen a wide variety of ways in which being perceived as affiliated or as likeable can improve your chances of achieving a positive outcome. In this next section we consider what specific action steps you can take to increase your influence over people and outcomes at work without having to resort to being everyone's best friend, or even behaving unethically.

Recognizing the opportunity to create affiliation

Imagine you are a mid-level employee in the local branch of a large international company. A senior manager from headquarters is making a regional visit. He or she is visiting the local market and meeting with the most senior people in your branch, although there will be a few opportunities to spend some minutes one-on-one with employees such as yourself.

Remarkably, you find yourself face-to-face and alone with that senior figure, whom you are meeting for the first time. That person asks you a generic question such as 'How is the job going?' What is your reply?

Given that you are unprepared to answer, your initial response will be a knee-jerk reaction. Many people will answer with an exclamation such as 'great!', or the equivalent in their usual terminology. However, once you have had the opportunity to collect your thoughts, a common follow-up response is for the employee to start describing a problem to that senior figure – for example, 'the main problem we are facing is a hold-up in approvals from the accounts department'. This is very normal behaviour – and one I have observed many times in different circumstances. It is also the direct opposite of skilfully applying Principle Three.

Consider what influence this interaction had on the senior figure. One likely outcome is that he or she raises the issue with the local managers (including yours) when re-joining them later that day. These local managers – who likely did prepare for the senior figure's visit – are now left in a defensive position because of your comment, which is not a way to win friends and influence people. Further, the senior figure will then consider that their responsibility towards the issue is now complete and has no particular reason to remember anything about you. They jet off into the sunset, while you return to the daily routine, now with the added problem of having irritated the head of the accounts department.

If you were the employee, how could you have seized this opportunity and applied your influencing skills to achieve a better outcome? As with all of the influencing principles outlined in this book, the biggest missed opportunity for most people is recognizing in advance that an opportunity to create positive affiliation, positive influence and positive outcomes will or might present itself. The second biggest missed opportunity is failing to prepare ahead of time to seize that moment, should it occur.

Create affiliation by highlighting a similarity

The number one technique for creating a sense of affiliation in a decision-maker is to highlight a real similarity between you. You will need to conduct research into the background and activities of the influence target to find suitable similarities. Make a list of anything you find that might lead to your being seen as similar. Something is better than nothing, but ideally, you are looking for:

1. **Positive factors:** Something that the person would be proud of or happy to acknowledge. This will have the dual effect of inducing a positive emotion that can be associated with you, at the same time as highlighting your similarity.

2. **Salient or unusual factors:** Ideally, features that are differentiating, something that puts you and them together in a category that is not – for example – shared by other job applicants or peers. Research shows the rarer the similarity you share, the stronger the affiliation effect.[29] People also seem to prefer a shared preference that was required deliberately instead of accidentally.

3. **Factors relatively more important to social identity:** Although we have seen that a sense of affiliation can be created even through sharing the experience of having electrodes stuck to your head,[7] recall that one key driver for in-group classification behaviour is reinforcing one's own sense of identity. As such, factors likely to be more closely related to a person's identity (e.g., we are both members of the Harley-Davidson Club) will create a stronger affiliation than something more transient (e.g., we both just flew from the same airport).

Table 3.1 provides examples of similarities of how you can evaluate the relative strength of similarities you find between yourself and the influence target.

TABLE 3.1: Examples to help you assess the relative strength of similarity factors

Example	Positive	Salient or Unusual	Important to Social Identity	Verdict
You both just returned from a holiday in Greece	Probably positive (if the holiday went well)	Salient if the holiday was recent for each of you and the location is unusual	Unlikely to be important to social identity	Better than nothing
You both studied at the same college	Positive if the person is proud of the college	Salient if it distinguishes you	Probably important to social identity	Good example
The person is from Singapore, and you lived there for three years	People are almost always proud of where they were born	Salient if you are meeting outside of Singapore. Even better if you actively chose to live in Singapore over other attractive locations	Likely to be important to social identity	Very good example
You have both volunteered to work on a charity project e.g. Habitat for Humanity or Red Crescent	People are almost always proud of their charity work	Likely to be salient because volunteering is not a common activity	Likely to be important to social identity because volunteer work often makes people feel good	Very good example

When should I do this similarity identification exercise?

You can do this exercise ahead of any important meeting or situation in which you want to influence a decision-maker – even when the person already knows you and your work. The perception of affiliation can change from context to context and – provided the similarity is highlighted in an appropriate manner – affiliation can be ramped up in the moment. You should certainly dedicate time to identifying similarities before you meet an influence target for the first time – such as a hiring manager, a new colleague or a potential client. If you have the person's name, you can likely find information online. If you do not have a name, consider whether or not you can ask for one, or perhaps work it out. On one recent occasion, I was asked to make a presentation to the regional CEO of a client's client. No one on my side could tell me the person's full name, but by tracking through email chains I was able to identify his first name as 'Richard'. That was sufficient for me to use internet searches to find the full name of a Richard with the right job title in the right country, and the full name was enough to bring up a detailed LinkedIn profile, as well as some industry news about some of Richard's recent initiatives in the community.

Carefully consider how to introduce the affiliating information appropriately

A crucial consideration in executing your influencing plan will be finding an appropriate moment and method for introducing the affiliating information in your interaction. The person you are meeting will probably be flattered if you heard from a mutual acquaintance that he or she ran the Berlin Marathon last year – and that you are considering doing something similar yourself. In contrast, it is not only creepy to mention that you searched for your influence target and discovered selfies of them and their dog: you are also likely to embarrass him or her. Above all, remember that your objective is to make the other person feel good, happy, and affiliated as well as respected – not awkward, stalked or intruded upon. Introducing the information about your affiliation must seem natural. Bringing it up in a manner that indicates you have thoroughly investigated him or her can leave you confined to the 'out-group' of 'scary people'.

Creating an affiliation by leveraging mutual contacts

Knowing the same people can also create affiliation: in a crowd of strangers, you will feel closest to the friend of a friend. Creating affiliation through mutual contacts follows the same parameters as creating affiliation through a similarity – for example, the more this mutual contact is liked or esteemed by the person you are meeting, the greater the positive affiliation that will be associated with you as a result of being linked to someone who is already liked. This is the same mechanism exploited in referral marketing, whereby people become more likely to buy a product or service based on the recommendation of a family member or friend.[30] Again, just as with affiliation through similarity, being able to identify any contact that you have in common is a good place to start. While you might not share a friend, have you ever worked in the same circles, or been taught by the same professor? Can you obtain a reference from someone the influence target knows – or someone with whom the influence target might feel affiliated because he or she graduated from the same school? Begin with any mutual reference points and do some investigation.

Create an affiliation by highlighting that you share the same goals

Let's revisit the example of an impromptu meeting with a senior figure in your company that was mentioned above. In this context it is likely that you would know the person's name and know of their visit in advance. You should also know (or be able to find out) what are the top priorities of that senior leader. You can create both a sense of affiliation and a memorable positive impression if you are prepared to highlight how you have contributed to that person's top priorities.

Imagine again this person asking you 'How is the job going?' If you had prepared, you could say 'Great! This month, I have added three new clients from the tech industry to our customer list. I know it's particularly important to you that we find more technology-based clients, so my team and I are doing our best to help the company achieve that goal.' Not only have you created a positive emotional experience, and an affiliation suggesting you are part of that person's team helping to achieve their goals, this is the kind of news that a senior person might include in a summary of a trip to your region – and that summary would likely be sent to other senior people. The senior figure may well remember your name. You might even be asked to create a chart, or a slide with details of your team's contribution. And that is the difference between a seized opportunity and a wasted one.

Creating liking vs creating relationships

Contrary to what you might expect, I am not going to give you blanket advice to simply aim to be highly liked by everyone at work. That would be a problematic goal because society holds men and women to different standards for being likeable, especially when women are successful at work.[31,32] Further, certain personality types – such as introverts, or people who fit the 'conscientious' quadrant of the DISC personality typology and who are thus more focused on tasks than on people – find it more difficult to invest the same amount of time as extroverts in social activities. Finally, I don't want to give you more reasons – on top of social media judgements and any natural variations in your own confidence – to spend any more time worrying about what other people think of you!

However, the science review we just covered provides important suggestions for steps you can take to increase your current likeability *relative to what it might otherwise be* without having to compromise on being competent, nor to feel obligated to say yes to everything that comes your way, nor to befriend everyone at the office. The actions suggested by this review acknowledge the human relationship side of working with people. We have seen that people like those who are similar to them, who like them first, who compliment them, give them attention or show care towards them. Hence, here are science-approved methods for creating positive relationships with co-workers:

1. **Ask your co-workers how their morning/day/meeting went.** Research has shown that even people lower in trust feel more cared for when asked about their day or their

other experiences on a regular basis by someone who
listens to their answers.[19]

2. **When listening to a colleague, paraphrase something
   he/she said.** Research shows that a paraphrased reflection
   is more effective than a simple acknowledgement in
   generating positive feelings about the listener.[33]

3. **Compliment people and use positive adjectives to
   describe others.** Be careful about the comments you
   make about other people. A phenomenon known as
   'spontaneous trait transference' describes the measured
   effect that people describing others become associated
   with the traits they are describing, despite the fact they are
   not describing themselves.[34] Hence, saying positive things
   about other people not only makes that other person feel
   good, the compliments you give will rub off on you in the
   minds of people listening in.

4. **Bring positive emotion rather than negative emotion
   to a meeting.** Emotion is contagious.[35] If you consistently
   emanate positive emotion then people around you will
   tend to feel more positive also – and people like to be
   around people who make them feel positive.

As highlighted above, there is no need to try to be everyone's best
friend. However, setting aside just 10 minutes per day to take one or
more of the four actions listed above will improve your relationships
with others and hence your influencing power in the workplace.

BETTER THAN YESTERDAY: HELPING YOURSELF USING THE PRINCIPLE OF AFFILIATION

In many professional situations it can be tempting to try to prove
our own value by finding fault in what other people have done. By
pointing out someone else's mistakes we are subtly communicating
that we know a better way and we can succeed where other people
have failed. This temptation can feel particularly strong when you
are new to a role or feeling insecure about your position.

Focusing on other people's mistakes might make you feel good – however, consider the habit you are creating. Instead of developing your long-term capability in building affiliation and relationships among your professional network, you are forming a habit of tearing people down rather than lifting them up. The longer this goes on, the more you will reduce rather than increase your overall social capital. And as you grow in seniority as well as competence, habits such as these run the risk of transforming you into other people's competent jerk.

ILLUSTRATION OF PRINCIPLE THREE (*AFFILIATION*)
FIGURE 3

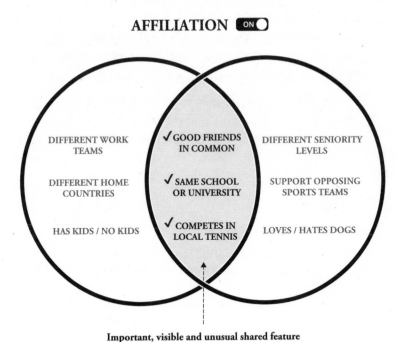

Important, visible and unusual shared feature

FIGURE 3: We are positively influenced by those whom we perceive as being like us, or a member of 'our group'. Your goal is to highlight similarities between you and the influence target.

Key takeaways

- Employees are influenced by co-workers they like in several ways: being more likely to seek them out, more likely to choose them as partners and also more likely to do their best work when working with them.

- We tend to like and be influenced by people who share similar characteristics to us, who like us first and who praise or compliment us (without unnecessary flattery).

- Being able to create a sense of affiliation between yourself and another person can help to tip decisions in your favour in a whole range of workplace scenarios.

- When meeting someone for the first time, set aside some reflective time to prepare for the meeting, to create positive affiliations and emotions. This is more likely to lead to them remembering your contribution positively and being inclined to agree with you.

- Be mindful to introduce information appropriately, depending on the scenario and the role/seniority of the person you are hoping to build affiliation with.

Principle Four

Value Framing (Because You're Worth It!)

Executive summary

Value framing increases your influencing power by modifying your audience's perception of worth. In the same way that an expense in one currency sounds more meaningful when expressed in another, you can make a benefit appear more valuable by expressing it in terms that have inherent power, or a price seem less significant by comparing it to something more expensive. There are three key sets of techniques you can use for value framing: choice of context, use of a comparison and value conversion. These techniques enable you to create the perception that an object is large or small, fast or slow, beneficial or risky. In the workplace, your ability to skilfully apply Principle Four will enable you to influence how others perceive the value of your project, the magnitude of your contributions, the importance of a decision or the size of a problem, as well as many other career-influencing dimensions.

HOW BIG IS AN APPLE?

Contrary to popular opinion, size isn't everything – context is. Let me give you an example. If an apple is placed next to a watermelon, it appears small. However, replace the watermelon with a cashew and the apple seems large. You do not need to change the size of the apple to change how it is perceived, you only need to change the contents of the fruit bowl!

L'Oréal's *because you're worth it* campaign was specifically designed to remind consumers that the cost of a lipstick is a small price to pay compared to the benefit of a radiant smile. Similarly, makers of high-end pet food remind you that their vet-designed products cost less than one apple per day – and who wouldn't spend that small amount each day on their best friend? Consumer goods companies such as L'Oréal and P&G teach brand managers the practice of value conversion: expressing one variable (like price) in terms of other values that are inherently powerful (such as health) in order to reframe how an object is perceived. Yet the power of the value-framing techniques we will examine here extends well beyond the pricing of branded items. Masterful use of context, comparison and conversion can influence the value, desirability, importance, size, risk, fear, likelihood, and cost that we associate with pretty much anything.

How we judge value

In the introduction to this book, I explained the concept of brain shortcuts by which our conscious understanding is biased through faulty data processing. It is such an important concept in all nine influence principles that it is worth re-explaining now you are part way into this book. In any given moment, our brains receive millions of individual bits of information, but we only have the mental capacity to pay attention to a small number of them. As a result, our brains operate as if they are running an underlying programme to classify stimuli in terms of how much they deserve conscious attention, sending the lucky winners to the forefront of our minds and ignoring everything else.[1] The truth is that as human beings, we don't have the mental capacity to consider every detail of a situation. While some stimuli – termed 'primary' stimuli in psychology – have inherent value to us because of their biological relevance (e.g., an electric shock that causes immediate pain), many stimuli derive most of their value from whatever information happens to be most easily available at the time. Hence, your evaluation or judgement of an object is determined by the particular measuring stick or evaluation framework that is easiest to use.

In this chapter, we will use the term 'Value Framing' for the techniques you can use to determine the measuring stick or framework through which your target audience makes an evaluation. We will classify Value Framing into three categories of actions you can apply in the workplace:

1. Choice of context or background
2. Use of a comparison set
3. Value conversion.

Each of these techniques influences people and outcomes by influencing how people perceive – and hence respond to – a situation.

CONTEXT IS A SUBTLE BUT POWERFUL TOOL

Context is a subtle but powerful manipulator. For example, people are more likely to want to buy common household brands (e.g. Red Bull or Apple Mac) when they see the product being used by characters in a feature they enjoy, than when they see the product in a dedicated commercial.[2,3] This power comes from the fact that these two different contexts affect the associations and assumptions that people make about that product – even though the product itself does not change. Research in both humans and animals tells us that the context within which a certain stimulus occurs changes how it is perceived, whether you are an adult human, a kindergartener, a Charles River rat[4] or even an ant.[5]

Although we are unlikely to notice in day-to-day interactions, we often make judgements about how others are feeling based as much on our perception of their situation as on how those people express themselves (or indeed, what they are actually feeling). An Italian study from the University of Parma demonstrated that subjects interpreted other people as feeling either happy or fearful when images of those people wearing neutral expressions appeared in a film sequence, suggesting that the person was looking at either happiness-inducing stimuli, such as kittens, or fear-inducing stimuli, such as spiders.[6] It doesn't matter that the person *could have* a crippling fear of cats (Ailurophobia) – fluffy kittens traditionally inspire joy, so the person watching them must be happy, mustn't they? Our perception is also affected by which details of a situation are accessible to us. For example, the character trait of 'honesty' can generate a positive impression of a fictional character when that honest person is described as returning a lost purse – but a negative impression when the honest person is described as telling a partner that he or she is fat.[7]

PEOPLE'S FEELINGS ARE ALSO AN IMPORTANT CONTEXT

In human interactions we should also consider people's emotional state as a form of context. If you ask your friends to tell you their greatest fears when you are sitting in broad daylight in a café, you will likely get a very different response from those they give to the same question in the middle of the dark woods at night. People who watch a television commercial during a programme that makes them feel happy rate the commercial more positively than people watching the same commercial during a programme that makes them feel sad.[8]

Further, current mood appears to bias perception by also affecting both attention and memory retrieval. A cohort of postgraduate students in a positive mood throughout an operations management class significantly outperformed a cohort who experienced a less positive mood during the same class when those two cohorts were given an impromptu learning and memory test two days later.[9] College students asked to remember the events of the previous week were better able to recall pleasant events when they were feeling happy, and unpleasant events when they were feeling sad.[10] In other words, if you want to influence people to perceive your project positively or to remember positive things about you, then find ways to ensure they are feeling happy at the time (feeding people candy seems to work).[11]

The overall takeaway is that by controlling the choice of context, the backdrop, or the ambient feeling in the room, you can differentially influence people's perception of the same item, proposal, or idea. This is an effective but also subtle approach to working with influence because people tend to be focused on the main message or object rather than its surroundings.

THE WORST THING THAT CAN HAPPEN IS...

After first appearing in the 1960s, there have been various iterations of an amusing fictional letter that a college student sends to her parents to update them on her news at the end of her first semester away.[12] In the version I use in my classes, the email seeks to reassure her mum and dad that she is 'almost better now' after she sustained fractures and a concussion when escaping a fire in her university residence and that she and her new fiancée will get married as soon as her syphilis clears up and before the baby starts to show. The letter finishes by stating that she did not go to hospital, she is not pregnant, and she does not have syphilis – but she will be receiving very low grades in some of her subjects.

Over several years of using this example with highly diverse cohorts of master's degree students from more than 120 different countries, I have never yet had to explain what the fictional student is attempting to do, nor how she expects this technique to work. This is an example of a technique we will label 'creating a comparison', through which you can influence others to perceive something as good or bad news, fast or slow, important or unimportant, based on what you compare it to.

The influencing power of a comparison derives from our frequent tendency to make evaluations that are relative rather than absolute.[5] For example, imagine you are being offered a new position at a new salary. Rather than evaluate the salary offer on its own terms as compensation for a specific role, you would likely evaluate that salary positively or negatively by comparing it with your current salary, or the salaries of your friends, or perhaps your parents at the same age.

In a clever experimental demonstration of this technique, a team of American researchers[13] approached college students walking alone on campus and asked them if they would be willing to give up a day of their time to accompany a group of young offenders on a trip to the zoo. Of all the people they approached, only 17 per cent agreed. Then they repeated the experiment with one variation: the college students were first asked to commit two hours of voluntary work per week for a minimum period of two years to counsel young offenders. None of the people interviewed agreed to this significant commitment. However, when these same people were then asked to accompany a group of young offenders on a 'day trip' to the zoo, more than 50 per cent of them agreed to it. Another memorable example of the influencing power of comparisons comes from a study of championship athletes who won silver and bronze medals. Researchers identified that those who won bronze medals were significantly happier than those who had won silver medals because bronze medallists perceived themselves as almost missing out on the podium (the positive side of a divide), whereas silver medallists saw themselves as missing out on attaining first place (the negative side of a divide).[14]

People consistently seek out relative benchmarks when making judgements of a wide variety of phenomena.[15,16,17] This approach may even be hard-wired in our evolutionary roots: Capuchin monkeys refuse to participate in tasks resulting in a cucumber reward after they witness another monkey get a better reward (grapes) for the same amount of work.[18] The resulting comparison-based evaluation of any one item is different from that which would be produced if there were no comparisons available.[19, 20]

AIM TO DETERMINE THE COMPARISON SET

The term 'comparison set' describes the set of reference points or benchmarks that people use to make these relative evaluations.

When conducting in-house research for P&G, my colleagues and I found that a shopper's first step when choosing a shampoo brand is to establish a relative comparison set. This involves excluding most of the numerous brands available in order to create a smaller and more manageable group of potential candidates. This process should sound familiar: it is the same procedure used by hiring managers to create a shortlist of applicants and is probably the approach you use when choosing a holiday location from all available options. In the case of shampoo shoppers, the comparison set typically involves three brands: the shopper's most frequent or usual brand, plus two alternatives they might consider if that brand offered a special promotion or a new product feature.*

Now that you know that people look for comparison sets to use in evaluating an idea, proposal or investment, your key to influencing these evaluations is providing an easily available comparison set that creates the perspective you are seeking. In general, if a comparison set includes several excellent examples, then a member of the set that is merely good will be perceived more negatively than if it were on its own. This is termed a 'negative contrast'. In contrast, a 'positive contrast' occurs when decision-makers are exposed first to a series of poor-quality examples: now, a good example will be rated more positively than if it were on its own.[20, 21]

The overall takeaway is that the technique of creating a comparison set influences how people perceive something by providing a measuring stick for evaluating it. If your measuring stick is in Michelin stars, your local restaurant might seem pretty lame; if it is in health violations, your local restaurant might be a stand-out performer. If you lost money for your company this year, but you can find a legitimate way to compare yourself to people who lost twice as much, well, maybe you are a strong performer...

---

*Interestingly, we also found that in some categories, such as jam, when people find it too difficult to reduce the selection available down to a preferred comparison set, they will report that the store does not have 'enough choice' no matter how many individual brands might actually appear on a shelf

Changing perception through value conversion

Imagine you have a relatively shy and modest friend who recently returned from a trip to London. You ask your friend about the holiday and he or she says they visited Buckingham Palace, then the Tower of London, then they participated in the London Marathon. Being polite, you say to your friend, 'Oh cool, how long did that take you?' Your friend replies, 'Two hours and 20 minutes. It was really hard.'

If – like 90 per cent of the population – you are not someone who runs long road races, this information will mean very little to you. You might say, 'Oh great, well done.' However, if you are a regular runner of long-distance road races, your mouth might fall open in shock as you realize that whether your friend is male or female, they will likely be asked to represent their country in marathon running at the next Olympic Games.

To communicate the power of this hypothetical marathon performance to my MBA class I ask attendees if they have ever been on a treadmill. Most people raise their hands. The average speed at which people jog on a treadmill is around seven minutes per kilometre. Next, I ask them to imagine that they ramp their treadmill up to a speed of three minutes and 20 seconds per kilometre, which is close to a flat-out sprint for a fit person. Finally, I ask them to imagine they remain on that treadmill, running at that same speed, until they have run just over 42 kilometres (or 2,110 times the length of a cricket pitch). Now they understand the value of running the London Marathon in two hours and 20 minutes.

Similarly, if you are attempting to influence people to reduce their daily energy usage, giving them feedback on their consumption in terms that are not automatically meaningful has almost no impact.[22] After all, if I can help you to save 1,000 kilowatt hours of energy, is that a lot? In her well-viewed TEDx Talk, Dr Jennifer Cross[23] explains that telling homeowners they have many gaps in their window and door frames does little to influence them to do anything. However, if those same homeowners are told they have a hole in their home the size of a basketball, you will see a dramatic improvement in the proportion of people who will act to fill those gaps and reduce energy consumption. In either case you are communicating the same information: the influencing power lies in the choice of units. In a nutshell, the technique of value conversion influences how people perceive something by careful choice of the terms in which it is expressed.

It is a frequent occurrence in the workplace that we allow things that we care about deeply (like the success of this project) to be expressed in units that are unrelatable, boring or easily overlooked. We say that our project is 'really important' instead of saying 'this project will bring in so much revenue we could buy everyone on the team a Ferrari' – which gets attention and communicates an intuitive sense of value (even if there is no chance the company will buy everyone a Ferrari).

Developing your skill in Value Framing: Differentiating and applying the three techniques

We will begin developing your skill in Value Framing by observing how your own perception of common situations changes in response to the three techniques.

Exercise 1: Examining the effects of the three techniques

Tables 4.1, 4.2 and 4.3 each provide an example of an experience that can change enormously in terms of perceived value using value-framing techniques. When examining each table consider the points listed below. If you make actual physical notes on your answers, you will learn more and are more likely to remember what you have learned.[24] Hence, you will get more out of the exercise.

1. **Perceive**: How does your own reaction to the situation change in relation to each of the value frames? Make notes on how your evaluation of the situation, your emotional

response and your likely behavioural reaction vary, depending on the information provided.

2. **Distinguish**: Be sure you can distinguish each of the three techniques and how they differ in execution when applied to the same situation.

3. **Observe**: Notice that these common situations have relatively low inherent value in the absence of the value-framing factors.

4. **Recognize**: You will see that every statement within each table could be true. In other words, the reality of the situation has not changed; all that has changed is the information available and hence, your perception.

First up, let's consider Table 4.1: Waiting in a queue for four hours. Whether you are in that queue on foot, in your car, or through a virtual process like a phone line, how could each of the three value-framing techniques be applied to influence your perception, your emotions and your reactions to the situation? What if you were one of the few people in the world who was lucky enough to wait in that queue, while many were not even allowed to join it?

TABLE 4.1: A four-hour wait in a queue perceived through the three Value-Framing lenses

Technique	Perceived as a Long Wait	Perceived as a Short Wait
Context or Background	Waiting at a doctor's office when your appointment time was over three hours ago	When you get to the front of the queue you will be given a life-saving vaccine not available elsewhere
Comparison Set	There is another 'VIP' queue in which people wait only five minutes	Yesterday, the average wait time was more than 10 hours
Value Conversion	Ten per cent of your working hours this week were spent waiting in this queue (four hours of 40)	Waiting in this queue comprised only 2 per cent of your total week (four hours of 168)

TABLE 4.2: Receiving a B grade on an Executive MBA assignment

Technique	Poor Performance	Strong Performance
Context or Background	You have a colleague who completed the degree programme before you. He or she said this course was pretty easy	You were having an extremely stressful time at work while taking this course in the evenings. At one point you thought you would not be able to submit any assignment at all
Comparison Set	The average grade across the whole class was a B+	Among students who were new to the subject (like you), the average grade was a C-
Value Conversion	You put in more hours of study than on other courses and got a worse result!	You now have a strong foundational understanding of an area that was completely new to you – and you will be able to apply your new knowledge for greater success at work

Second, let's imagine you are an Executive MBA student (Table 4.2). Midway in your career, you signed up to a part-time degree programme to improve your skills and move further towards a general management role. You receive feedback on a major assignment for one of your core courses: you scored an overall grade of B.

In our final example, your contract is renewed with your company, but at a salary rate that is 10 per cent below what you were paid for the past year (Table 4.3). Is that good or bad? Well, it depends on the value frame.

Exercise 2: Your turn to apply the three Value-Framing techniques

Now it is your turn to generate value frames using each of the three techniques. **Do not attempt to mix the three approaches together**. If you are learning a new tune on the piano, you need to be able to distinguish each chord separately before you can bring them together in a sequence. In the same way, in order to gain skill mastery, it is

TABLE 4.3: Your new contract is at a salary rate 10 per cent lower than last year

Technique	Bad News	Good News
Context or Background	If this trend continues, you will be earning 20 per cent less by December next year	The industry is doing badly. Without salary reductions your job might have to be cut altogether
Comparison Set	Your two colleagues didn't receive a salary reduction	Your salary is still in the top 25 per cent for roles in this industry
Value Conversion	You just worked 12 months to go backwards in income	The amount you are paid is very good given how much you like the work. In fact, if you didn't know otherwise you would probably do this job for half the pay

important that you can distinguish the three techniques and develop the ability to use each of them independently long before you can consider a multi-tool approach. This is the only way to be sure you are following an effective methodology to generate your approach. Hence, you should be able to create a **Comparison Set** approach to value framing that is strictly and distinctly different from your **Value Conversion** approach and different again from your **Context**-based approach. Imagine you are being awarded grades for your efforts – because if you were in my class, you would be given grades!

In Exercise 2, a manager asks one of his or her direct reports to work on an additional project in a team composed of people from other departments, including two senior managers. The project is outside the scope of the direct report's current role and all meetings will take place online in the evening because of the geographical location of team members. Is this a good offer that gives the person a chance to expand his or her network and skills, or a terrible burden, involving doing more work for no extra pay? In this exercise, you must drive those perceptions by completing Table 4.4 using each of the three techniques independently.

TABLE 4.4: Value Framing the opportunity to work on an additional project with a new team

Technique	Good News	Bad News
Context		
Comparison Set		
Value Conversion		

To view our answers to this exercise and compare your own, go to dramandanimonpeters.com

PLANNING TO INFLUENCE PEOPLE AND OUTCOMES USING PRINCIPLE FOUR

Now that you have knowledge of the techniques and have begun to develop your ability to apply them, let's examine how you can use value framing to influence people and outcomes in common work-related situations. Value framing is particularly valuable as a technique in the workplace because often the most powerful and influential aspects of our work are exactly those that we forget to mention, or that we consider obvious (when to others they are not), so we leave them unsaid.

Maximizing the value of your results and achievements

Context is a good tool to start with when aiming to maximize the value of your achievements. If two people swam 100m in the sea yesterday, it was a much bigger achievement for the person who has been deathly afraid of the sea for years and who worked towards that goal step by step, than for the person who grew up next to the sea and regularly swims much further distances in it. If one student leader started a club that attracted 100 members, and another started a club that attracted only 30 members, the latter might be perceived as a better result if the first club were the drinking and partying club, and the second club was a community volunteering club.

As a recruitment interviewer at P&G, I advised candidates to describe their past achievements using the acronym Context – Action – Result. If you search online, you will find blogs and popular articles that carry similar advice and use either the C-A-R acronym or a comparable model for structuring narratives about past accomplishments. **Context** – setting the scene – is necessary for clear and concise storytelling because aspects of the situation that seem obvious to you will not be obvious to others. More importantly, however, careful placement of the **action** you took and the **result** you achieved within a specific context or background will serve to communicate the magnitude or relevance of each achievement. First, examine the examples in Table 4.5, then attempt to apply the approach by writing three of your own achievements within a context that amplifies their value. Again, notice that both versions of the example can be true.

TABLE 4.5: Using context or background to value frame your achievements

Example	Better Example
I expanded the list of customers subscribing to our newsletter	I expanded our number of email subscribers by 600 per cent (from 500 to 3,500) without increasing spend from our social media budget
I organized a popular volunteer event	The members of this community had never participated in a volunteer event, so the concept was new to them. Through a series of social media posts, I attracted 50 people to attend the first event, which is twice what the team had expected, given the small size of the company
I ran training sessions for my colleagues in Excel-based data analysis	I identified a bottleneck in our department: around one-third of my colleagues did not know how to use Excel to perform our monthly sales analysis. I gained management agreement to provide a targeted training session. Now everyone in our department uses Excel for this purpose. Sales analyses are completed faster and with fewer errors

When you initially begin listing your achievements, it will be much easier for you to generate items that resemble those in the first column of Table 4.5 rather than those in the second column. Progressing from the left column to the right column takes practice – but it is work from which you will benefit, so you should make the effort and keep challenging yourself until you have crafted some masterful backdrops to showcase your achievements.

Where did you get that data?

Upon reading the examples in the right column of Table 4.5 you might have wondered how someone would access the data used in these examples – such as the fact that one-third of employees did not know how to use Excel. Although you won't like the answer (see Principle Five: *Effort*), the most reliable method of having data such as these is to anticipate the need for such data and collect it yourself. This observation leads us neatly from the role of context or background to how we might use **value conversion** in presenting our achievements.

Start by identifying the variables that have the highest inherent value to the influence target with whom you will communicate. Whether that stakeholder is your current manager, a hiring interviewer, a board or panel of judges, or a customer audience, make a list of the top 10 factors, variables or commodities that will strike them as valuable or powerful. Now choose one past achievement and consider how to make the appropriate value conversion: express the outcome of your achievement in the units of those powerful variables. Again, Table 4.6 provides examples of what your list of achievements might look like before and after applying value conversion.

After reviewing Table 4.6 and working at designing methods of expressing your own achievements using value conversion you will likely identify metrics and data that it would be handy to have readily available – such as attendees' self-rated levels of engagement before and after your initiative. With forethought, data like this is not difficult to capture and can easily be obtained by creating a short survey or rating scale and then asking attendees to complete it. The key to success is to develop your ability to identify factors or variables that carry inherent value and then plan in advance to capture that data as you go about executing your responsibilities.

TABLE 4.6: Using value conversion to value frame your achievements

Example	Better Example
I expanded the list of customers subscribing to our newsletter	I extended the list of customers subscribing to our newsletter. Now over half of our subscribers are senior managers with budget responsibility
I implemented an initiative that was well received. People in the office/group/class liked it	I implemented an initiative that resulted in an increase in employees' self-rated levels of engagement and sense of purpose within their team
I ran a short training programme for my colleagues	I ran a training programme for my colleagues, who estimated afterwards that the new procedure would save them up to a day of processing time for each report they create

Framing your achievements with a comparison set

Finally, you also have an opportunity to improve how your results are perceived by providing a statement of results that automatically includes comparison to less successful outcomes. Table 4.7 provides two such examples.

TABLE 4.7: Using a comparison set to value frame your achievements

Example	Better Example
I received a B in marketing	I was in the top 15 per cent of my class on a highly competitive marketing programme. Many people were unable to pass the course
My team's sales results were 5 per cent higher than in the previous period	Across the western region, sales averaged 20 per cent lower than the previous period, while my team's sales were 5 per cent higher than last period

Which one of these Value-Framing techniques should you choose?
The answer to this question is simple: whichever one most effectively improves how your achievements or ideas are positioned. You have three tools at your disposal. Apply each of them in turn to your list of results and achievements, then select the best examples across all of those you have generated. You might find that one result looks better when you apply value framing, while another looks better when you choose a specific comparison set. The technique is simply the route to the result.

INFLUENCING PERCEPTION OF A BUSINESS ISSUE OR A PROJECT TO WIN SUPPORT

Value conversion is an essential step
In the face of seemingly conclusive data identifying our perilous journey towards climate change, or the preventative role of mask-wearing in stopping the spread of infectious diseases, why do groups of people vehemently disagree? Is it simply because some people are dispassionate, logical subscribers to science, while others don't know about or don't understand, the data? If that were the case, then there would be a strong relationship between changing opinions on these issues and simply increasing people's understanding of scientific data, but that relationship is weaker than you might think.[25]

One key driver of divergent positions is that people do not evaluate data in the same way: information is interpreted through a process akin to value conversion – that is, in terms of values that matter to the individual. Hence a meta-analysis of studies on factors that drive public adherence to quarantine measures recommends it is not enough to provide information: governments must provide that information in a way that increases the perceived benefits of engaging in quarantine, as well as the perceived risk of contracting a virus.[26] In the same way, when you present an issue or a project to a manager or a committee in the hope of gaining support, it is not enough to simply present 'the facts' as you see them. In order to exert influence and persuade others, you must carefully consider the values in which these facts are expressed.

A key first step in winning support, is to recognize the need to restrain yourself from listing all the information you can think of about why the issue is important – because the reasons you can think of are expressed in values that are important to *you*. Simply inundating a target with more information expressed in values the target does not care about will render you more annoying, not more persuasive. As per the section on presenting your achievements using value conversion, attempt to put yourself into the perspective of your audience and draft out a list of the top factors or commodities that you believe your audience will find inherently valuable. How can you express the importance of this project in those terms, while still being truthful?

When your audience is large and diverse
If your audience is a large or diverse department, cohort or meeting room of people, start with what you know they have in common. At a foundational level, almost all humans care about receiving rewards, or increasing their success or status, and in general the bigger and more immediate such rewards, the more influential they will be in persuading people to care. For example, if you want your fellow MBA students to support your lobby for a particular career coach at the university, you will be more influential if you tell them 'this career coach has a high success rate in helping graduates identify jobs that they love' instead of 'this person is supposed to be a great career coach'. If everyone comes from the same team, then audience members may have a common value in the success of that team. Hence:

'This is a very costly issue'
becomes
'The cost of this issue is so high it could wipe out all the good results generated by our team this year'

When your audience is a senior manager in a specific department or company
If your audience is a specific senior manager or leader, a little investigative research can help you to identify the core values

of the company or the current goals of the department. For example, if you were seeking support for implementing an IT infrastructure project at Procter & Gamble, it is easy to uncover that the company expresses its primary purpose as 'improving the lives of the world's consumers'.[27] Senior people in P&G will be thoroughly familiar with this concept and so stating the value of your IT intervention as 'improving the lives of your employees by reducing the stress and complexity of essential daily tasks' will be more persuasive than your presentation on 'a more efficient IT system'.

When your audience is someone you know well
If you have worked or interacted with this person previously, prepare by considering what you know of their values and what has motivated them in the past. If you want to persuade someone you know to work with you on a project, consider carefully how to express the importance of the project in values that have previously mattered to them – for example, 'this project is going to involve a lot of fun activities' or 'this project gives you the chance to work with your favourite manager' or 'the other team members speak highly of your expertise'. Of course, none of these statements is likely to influence someone into joining a project that is easily identifiable as a very bad idea, but all of them increase your persuasive power and will tip the scales in your favour.

When you have the psychological profile details of your audience
Some very interesting experiments have identified that personality profiles can affect what values have the most power of persuasion over certain clusters of people. For example, adult Americans classified as 'Extroverts' were strongly influenced by an advertisement stating: 'With XPhone, you will always be where the excitement is' whereas those classified as 'Neurotic' were more influenced by the statement 'Stay safe and secure with the XPhone'.[28] Unless you have deep personal knowledge of your influence target – or you can whip out a quick personality test ahead of your influence attempt – I would suggest leaving these concerns aside until 1) you are ready

for advanced training in Value Framing, and 2) I have written the next book in this series.

Controlling the comparison set within the meeting or the presentation

Decisions to provide support or budget for a particular project will be heavily affected not only by the value of the terms in which the project is expressed, but also by the comparisons with other projects that decision-makers will automatically seek. If you do not prepare to present a comparison set to your audience, they will create their own, and you will have no control over the perception of your project as valuable or expensive, important or unimportant.

To apply the comparison set technique to winning support or resources for your project:

1. **Identify the big and small:** Identify the elements of your message that you wish to amplify and the elements you wish to minimize.
2. **Select comparison sets:** Select a relevant comparison set that will make the positives look big (like an apple next to a walnut) and a comparison set that will make the negatives look small (like an apple next to a watermelon).
3. **Plan the discussion:** Plan to lead the conversation so that discussion centres first around the positives and only secondly around the negatives. This step includes the advantage of focusing the most attention on an evaluation framework in which your project looks strong, as well as the potential for decision fatigue, whereby tired decision-makers find it easier to agree than to carefully consider all the data.[29] Refer to Principle Nine (*Execution*) to learn the importance of practising what you want to say aloud *before* you go live.

The ideal approach to persuading others to support your project is to be able to apply all three value-framing techniques in a short presentation. To illustrate, if you were looking for budget allocation to offer all employees a training in implicit bias, you might begin with the context of mass dissatisfaction over racial inequalities in the workplace and how this sentiment affects morale, as well as the company's reputation with stakeholders (Context). You might express the value of the training in terms of demonstrating commitment to employees, as well as developing their expertise in overcoming inherent bias to identify true high performers who produce the best results (Value Conversion). Having amplified the positives of this proposal, you might then minimize the price by comparing the cost of this training per employee (at $X per person) to the cost of a much more expensive training ($XXX per person) or losing disenfranchised but capable employees (at $XXXX per year) or even the cost of negative publicity potentially ($XXXXX). These costs form your Comparison Set.

BETTER THAN YESTERDAY: IMPROVING YOUR MENTAL OUTLOOK USING VALUE FRAMING

Reframing a problem or an upsetting situation in a manner that casts it in a more positive light is a technique used in therapy to help participants improve their mental outlook, feel better and potentially take action to solve problems. When a situation is perceived in a negative manner, it can induce stress or other adverse emotions and lead to ongoing avoidance behaviour. Re-framing a situation so it can be seen from a different point of view can help you feel better and might even suggest new actions or approaches that can make things better. So, for example, a therapist might enable you to redefine a problem as a challenge: 'problem' tends to induce negative energy, whereas a 'challenge' can seem more energizing.[30]

What problems are you facing today or this week that could be re-framed from problems into challenges that you can overcome?

ILLUSTRATION OF PRINCIPLE FOUR
(*VALUE FRAMING*) FIGURE 4

FIGURE 4: Our perception of value varies according to comparisons. An apple seems small when placed next to a watermelon. The same apple appears large when compared to a cashew.

Key takeaways

- Research shows that our perception of common situations changes in response to value-framing techniques – choice of context, use of comparison set and value conversion.

- By controlling the choice of context, backdrop, or the ambient feeling in the room, you can differentially influence people's perception of the same item, proposal, or idea.

- Choice of context involves providing a background that affects perception, such as when a branded products appears in a movie (compared to the same product in a commercial).

- The technique of creating a comparison set influences how people perceive something by providing a measuring stick for evaluating it.

- Value conversion involves influencing how people perceive something by careful choice of the terms in which it is expressed. Too often in the workplace, we allow things we care deeply about to be expressed in units that are unrelatable for others.

- Remember that people do not evaluate data in the same way. They interpret information in terms of values that matter to them.

- When setting out your achievements or ideas in order to influence others, be sure to consider the context in which you frame them, what factors carry inherent value, and what kind of comparisons you can make. Choose whichever techniques give you the best results on a case-by-case basis.

Principle Five

Effort (Make It as Easy as Possible)

Executive summary

It is well documented that humans generally take the easiest, lowest-effort pathway to achieve the outcome they seek. Whether the effort involved is physical or mental, the more difficult it is to do something, the less likely it becomes that people will do it. Our default attempts to influence others rarely take this into account. Hence, it is a common pitfall in daily work-related interaction that people generally create the opposite dynamic, making high-effort requests of those who have low inclination to help. In this chapter you will learn to evaluate influence attempts in terms of *effort dynamics*. Once you can identify effort dynamics in workplace situations, you will be able to adjust those dynamics to increase the likelihood that people reply to your emails, agree to help you, comply with your requests, and accept your invitations – whatever your position in the organization.

LIFE ON EASY STREET

Have you ever found yourself returning to a coffee stand or supermarket that you don't really like simply because its location is so ridiculously convenient? Or entering the highlighted options on a screen interface without paying attention to the labels on those buttons? Have you been tempted to watch the movie instead of reading the book, or jaywalk instead of waiting at the lights? If you have answered 'yes' to any of these examples, then the good news is that you are perfectly normal. In areas of human behaviour ranging from attention, creativity and thinking to actual bodily exertion, we behave as if our brains and bodies are running an underlying programme designed to conserve as much mental and physical effort as possible. Once you understand this principle – and can recognize it in action in daily dynamics – you will be able to use tools of influence that you never realized existed.

ASSUME EVERYONE IS LAZY, UNLESS THEY HAVE A GOOD REASON NOT TO BE

In the 1940s, the linguist George Kingsley Zipf described a tendency in human language for people to minimize the effort involved in using words while maintaining an acceptable level of communication.[1] Zipf demonstrated there was an inverse relationship between the length of a word and the frequency with which it is used. He also gave examples of long phrases that became truncated over time, presumably so that people could save on syllables. These same trends can be reproduced today in experimental studies of artificial language and coding.[2] Moreover, the use of acronyms that reduce the effort required to type or speak has continued to rise in business, science and even medicine despite ample evidence that they frequently worsen communication.[3,4,5] In fact, Zipf went further, proposing that all human behaviour followed a 'principle of least effort' in which people always take the approach that involves the least amount of exertion to accomplish any task. While this is not true in every instance for every person, it is widely accurate for most people most of the time. In simple terms, if you assume that everyone is as lazy as possible unless given a very good reason to behave otherwise, you will be right more often than not.

In extreme cases even very good reasons may not spur people into action. Archaeological research on the early human *Homo erectus* suggests that the species' extreme laziness could be one of the key reasons it went extinct.[6] A scientist studying one of their campsites commented that the stone tools they used were made from materials found at camp, although better-quality materials were just a short distance away: 'They knew it was there, but because they had adequate resources they seem to have thought, "why bother?"'[7] The study concludes that they may have been wiped out because, as the environment around them became drier and more hostile, 'they really don't seem to have been pushing themselves' to work any harder.

The tendency to take the easiest, most direct route recurs frequently in the behavioural patterns of both individuals and groups. For example, computer scientists are able to predict the movement pattern of pedestrians in confined spaces quite accurately just by identifying the routes from one location to another that represent the minimum caloric energy expenditure for every individual.[8] The assumption that, on average, people will choose an option that is easy instead of one that is more beneficial but more effortful is at the foundation of Nudge Theory – part of the work for which Richard Thaler and Cass Sunstein won a Nobel Prize in Economics.

To illustrate, imagine you are a public health official with the goal of reducing obesity in the population at large. A logical approach to influencing people's behaviour might be to design a series of public health announcements about the role of junk food in creating poor health and a campaign of warning labels on unhealthy food. In other words, a logical method of influencing seems to be providing information that gives people lots of very good reasons for changing their eating habits.* At first glance, this rational approach might seem sensible, but consider how much effort this approach requires from members of the public – first in paying attention to the information, second in deciding what foods

---

*We will revisit the influencing power of *supposedly* good reasons again in Principle Six (*Reasoning*)

to choose as alternatives and finally in locating those foods and continuing to choose them over an extended period. According to Nudge Theory, you will be much more successful without the need to explain anything or convince anyone if you simply make it extremely easy to find healthy food and much more difficult to find unhealthy food.[9]

OUR BRAINS ARE PRE-PROGRAMMED TO AVOID EFFORT

While Nudge Theory may appear to offer opportunities to nudge the population into behaviours that are good for them, one can also nudge people into behaviours that don't make sense for them just by making that behaviour easy to choose. Imagine you give a bucket of stale popcorn to a movie-goer who later tells you they didn't like the taste. As rational humans we expect that unless a person were starving, he or she would avoid eating something they don't like the taste of. Not so. Once researchers were able to get the two-week-old popcorn into people's hands, they ate around a quarter of what they were given.[10] It is simply easier to conform with the normative and thus expected behaviour of eating the popcorn in front of you while watching a movie than it is to rationally consider whether or not you truly enjoy eating it.

In fact, our brains go so far as to change our perception of reality in order to help us take the least-effort option. In a study conducted by Japanese, Canadian and British scientists, women aged 18 to 38 with normal vision were required to watch a series of moving dots on a screen and judge whether the dots appeared to be moving to the left or right.[11] They were asked to express their judgement by manipulating a lever to the left or right, in line with the direction of the dots. What they did not know is that the researchers randomly assigned a directional load such that it was harder to move the lever in one direction than the other. Participants' responses were significantly biased by the directional load they were given – in other words, when pushing to the right was harder, participants were more likely to judge the direction of the dots as moving to the left, and when pushing to the left was harder, they were more likely to judge the dots as moving to the right. The respondents were not consciously aware of the differences in force required and were truly convinced that the dots were moving in the direction that required less effort to report. The extra effort in pushing the lever changed what participants believed they saw – thanks to human brains that run an underlying programme designed to avoid physical effort.

We also avoid mental effort

Just as our brains are programmed to reduce our physical effort, they are also programmed to avoid mental effort. In his book *Thinking, Fast and Slow*, the behavioural economist Kahneman described mental activities as falling into one of two categories:[12] System One thinking that is easy, involves little effort and can be largely unconscious (such as scrolling through a feed on your phone, or reading the back of a cereal box), and System Two thinking that is mentally demanding and requires energy and attention to process information (such as solving a complex equation or wading through a textbook for a specific example). People's capacity for attention and effortful thinking is limited[13] and so they act to conserve this kind of mental activity for times when they really need it, or when they want the outcome badly enough to expend effort for it.

As an example, you can probably recall a time when you landed on a webpage or a YouTube video in search of a specific answer. If the webpage contained a long block of continuous text, or the video began with a generic introduction, it is likely you didn't waste many seconds before returning to the search engine to look for something simpler that got to what you needed faster. Similarly, a study of online shopping found that at least 20 to 30 per cent of carts are abandoned either because the purchase process involved too many steps or because it required users to create an account.[14] If you want someone to take an action (such as buying your product), you should make that action as easy as possible for them.

'SATISFICING' IS OUR KEY TECHNIQUE FOR ACQUIRING INFORMATION AND MAKING DECISIONS

Information-seeking is another area of human behaviour heavily affected by effort conservation – and highly relevant to influence. In general, people who are looking for information stop *as soon as minimally acceptable results are found*. This means they choose easy-to-use, simple information over more complicated or harder-to-access information, *even when they know that the simpler information is less accurate*.[15] Indeed, the term 'Satisficing' has been coined by scientists to make it easy to describe this minimally-good-enough decision-making behaviour.[16] The fact that people are unwilling to invest time and energy to access information that they acknowledge is of better quality is a prime example of effort conservation at work and helps to explain how accounts of current events or homemade remedies that are largely inaccurate (although minimally plausible) end up being circulated widely online. This has been exacerbated since the invention of 'share' buttons availed social media users of the opportunity to reach online communities by re-posting someone else's post, rather than making the effort to write something original.

As a behavioural pattern, you can expect that people will generally make a good enough decision to meet their needs, rather than the best possible decision out of all possible options. For example, consider the process you use when deciding which hotel to stay in when on holiday. Rather than make an extensive comparison between every possible hotel, it is more likely you obtain just enough information to feel that you are making a good decision. Satisficing seems perfectly reasonable in this context, doesn't it? However, consider that hiring managers who receive more applications than they need for an available position will exhibit the same behavioural pattern. When you write your application, you might erroneously believe that the recipients will treat it 'fairly', performing a thorough evaluation of every single resume. In fact, whether or not the hiring manager is consciously aware of the process, he or she will stop putting effort into searching for new information as soon as they are satisfied that they have a shortlist of enough good candidates to meet their needs.

ACCEPT THAT 'LAZY' IS ACTUALLY JUST NORMAL

Given that people act as if intrinsically programmed to conserve energy, attempts to avoid effort will undoubtedly be part of your workplace. Although I have suggested you will understand Principle Five better if you imagine that everyone around you is lazy, this does not mean that your co-workers deserve to be labelled as 'lazy' or 'slothful'. In fact, a more fitting label is 'normal'.

If you expect that it is normal for co-workers to avoid effort, then you will be less emotionally affected by someone's failure to respond to your request. Instead of asking 'why didn't they respond?' which leaves you to invent your own reasons, you might ask instead 'how much effort did I request?' Once you identify effort dynamics, adjust the dynamics of your requests to minimize effort and thus maximize the likelihood people will comply.

LEARN TO IDENTIFY EFFORT DYNAMICS IN YOUR WORKPLACE

What does 'effort' look like at work?

At this stage you are armed with a good science-based understanding of the principle of effort, and you can recognize that humans are programmed to conserve both physical and mental effort. To make best use of this understanding, you will need to recognize what counts as effort in a workplace context.

For example, reading an email or written message is an effort and that effort increases when the message is long or complex. Replying to an email is also effort, which again increases if the author is required to be creative or analytical or must obtain information just to respond. The perceived effort involved in both reading and replying to an email can be affected by how many other demands the recipient has on their time because we also act to conserve our attention and there is effort involved in diverting attention from one activity to another. That effort might also be put in the 'too high' category if the topic is not relevant or otherwise valuable to the reader. Once you see activities in the workplace through the lens of the effort each one requires, you will become much better at applying Principle Five to the situations you want to influence.

Factors that reduce the effort required to read an email

The mental effort involved in processing any communication – whether a spoken message, written report, data table or presentation – will vary considerably depending on how that communication is constructed and presented to the reader. For the purposes of workplace messages, there are several key factors that affect the readability of your text:

1. **Relevance of the topic:** Changing focus from one topic to the next requires effort. Therefore, the more your topic naturally attracts the attention of the reader, the lower the effort involved for someone to read it. There are two types of relevance for our purposes:

    I. **Relevant to current needs**: If your topic is immediately relevant to the current needs or most important business deliverables of the reader, they will probably be thinking about it already. Hence, less effort is involved in having to redirect their attention.

    II. **Relevant to perceived reward**: As we will discuss further in Principle Eight (*End-Goal Focus*), people's attention is easily diverted to any topic they might perceive as being linked to a reward[17] – in this case, messages about holidays, bonuses, promotion, etc.

2. **Shorter sentences**: Researchers who developed formulae for measuring overall text readability identified that the average length of sentences is a significant factor. According to Flesch, one of the leading researchers in this area, text becomes difficult to read once the average number of words in the sentences exceeds 21.[18] Text with

sentences averaging 17 words is 'standard' in readability
and those with sentences averaging 14 words tend to be
'fairly easy'. Of course, it matters a great deal exactly what
words are included in the sentence! Nonetheless, as a rule,
shorter sentences require less effort.

3. **Simpler, more familiar words**: Replacing sophisticated or
   technical terms with simpler words generally makes a text
   easier to read, as does using terminology or models that
   are familiar to the reader.[19]

4. **Structured text**: Text requires less effort to read when
   it is broken into shorter (vs longer) blocks. This is true
   particularly when the shorter blocks are placed into an
   information hierarchy that moves from general to specific
   points.[20] In this way, the structure of the text feeds the
   reader with one point at a time so that understanding
   is made easier. In contrast, when a reader is faced with
   long blocks of unbroken text, he or she must figure out
   for themselves where the separate points occur. Correct
   grammar and effective headings, together with lists and
   bullet points where appropriate, also reduce effort for
   the reader.

5. **Targeted focus**: An email is easier for a reader to process
   when it focuses on just the most important or highest
   value information instead of multiple topics of varying
   importance. Avoid the temptation to lump several topics
   together. What is most important? Start with that. You
   can always discuss the less important issues later. For now,
   your goal is to influence people to read your mail.

Exercise 1: Analyzing emails in terms of the effort involved in reading them

In this exercise you will develop your ability to detect the
effort level involved in reading a message. To start the exercise,
select the last three emails you received that were originated
by the sender (i.e., they were not responses to a message you

TABLE 5.1: Evaluating emails in terms of the effort required to read them

Factor	Effort Score Per Factor				
	1 Very high	2 High	3 Neutral	4 Low	5 Very low
1 Relevance of topic					
2 Shorter sentences					
3 Simple and familiar words					
4 Structured text					
5 Targeted focus					

had sent someone). Starting with just one email, use Table 5.1 above to give the message a score out of five on each of the factors listed. Next, sum the scores across all factors to give each email a reading effort score out of 25. The higher the score, the easier the message is to read. Repeat this exercise for all three emails you've chosen, and then review their relative reading effort scores. What is the range of scores across those examples? Which one requires the most effort to read? And the least effort? Remember, your brain is sensitive to even small increments in mental effort (as per the lever-pushing experiment), so small differences in scores can be relevant. If an email is not read at all, it has no influencing power.

How much work is that? Detecting effort dynamics in workplace interactions

The next step is to develop your ability to see the effort dynamics involved in interactions. We will start by evaluating some behaviours you might have seen, or even done yourself at work. Once you see those behaviours differently, you will be in a better position to move onto the final stage, which is adjusting the effort dynamics so you can have greater influence over people and outcomes in your professional life.

Exercise 2: Identify the effort dynamics in common workplace requests

Table 5.2 lists common requests that one person might make of another. On the surface, the asker's request might seem very reasonable. The request is probably important to the person

TABLE 5.2: Examples of common requests in the professional world

Request (Influence Attempt)	Estimated Time Required of Requester	Estimated Time Required of Receiver
1 **Reference letter:** Please may I ask you to write a recommendation letter to support my application to a master's degree programme? A reference letter is an essential part of my application. You can find the link to what is required attached to this mail.		
2 **Position enquiry:** I am writing to you as a highly esteemed person at your company. I would like to explore what opportunities are available at your organization. Please can we meet to discuss this?		
3 **Job application:** I am very interested in the position you have advertised. I have attached my CV and hope you will find that I am suitable for this role.		
4 **Input request:** I have attached a detailed plan of our proposal to the client and would welcome any input you may have.		
5 **Meeting request:** We have a meeting with the client. We would like you to attend the call to provide your expertise.		
6 **Advice request:** I am hosting an event and I was wondering how I should prepare. Any tips or suggestions from your side would be highly appreciated.		

who does the asking. However, there are always effort dynamics involved when making requests of others – and these dynamics will determine what people do.

For Exercise 2, consider the amount of effort required for the requester to make the request in contrast with the effort that would be required if the receiver were to execute that request. In essence, the requester has simply written a few sentences to ask a favour, whereas complying with the favour would require substantially more work. Your task is to provide some degree of benchmark for the contrast by giving your best estimate of the amount of time involved in the actions of the two parties (assuming the receiver complies). You will have an opportunity to get some feedback on your answers later in the chapter.

Influencing people and outcomes using the Principle of Effort

Making requests of others at work

Asking other people to do things for you is common workplace behaviour. One study of 200 Americans who had been in their current jobs for at least six months demonstrated that, when asked to do so, every one of them could recall instances in which they had attempted to influence people downwards, sideways or upwards in the organization to obtain help, advice, support or resources.[21] The behaviours described in Table 5.2 are common examples of the type of requests people make of each other in the workplace. I have received many such requests in each of the different countries and companies where I have worked and from people of many different nationalities.

Most of the time, people in the professional world will at least ask for what they want politely. Sometimes they will also attempt to use influencing tactics such as stating that it would be an honour if the recipient would help them. One further frequently used tactic is to make a personal appeal underlining just how much the requester needs the receiver to execute the request: in essence, asking for a favour.

Being polite or complimentary can certainly result in a request being viewed more favourably than one that is not expressed in such a way. However, are these sorts of approaches strong enough to persuade someone to exert significant effort on your behalf? Not often. One study of influencing attempts in the workplace estimated that personal appeals such as asking for favours was an approach more likely to result in **resistance** than commitment.[22] A recent meta-analysis of 49 independent studies from across the globe showed that although there was a positive relationship between personal appeals and achieving the desired outcome, the effect was small.[23]

If personal appeals are not particularly successful, why do people persist in using them? You can find the answer in Principle Five itself. Asking someone for something you want from them is the easiest way to try to get what you want. The approach *can* work – after all you have a better chance of getting what you want by asking for it than by not asking for it – but it's not the greatest approach.* The goal of this book is to enable you to do better than the average approach.

Changing the effort dynamics to increase your chances

The principle of effort enables us to make some fairly reliable predictions about what people are most likely to do in any circumstance. Statistically, they are most likely to do whatever is the easiest approach to meeting their needs. They are most likely to resist forces requiring them to expend physical and mental effort. They are most likely to conserve physical and mental effort unless they have a good reason for expending it. They will be far more inclined to exert effort for things they want, rather than things *you* want.

It is a common pitfall in daily work-related communication that people generally create the opposite dynamic, making substantial effort requests of those who have low inclination to help for the

---

* *See also* Principle Six (*Reasoning*) for an explanation of when simply asking for help can be effective

reasons provided. If your emails go unanswered, or your requests are unsuccessful, this could certainly be the reason behind that outcome.

The first step in manipulating the effort dynamics is to change your own perspective. Instead of thinking about what you want someone to do, and then trying to figure out how you can cleverly brainwash them into doing that, ask these questions to yourself instead:

Question 1: What is the least effort/most essential step that I truly need from the influence target?

Question 2: How can I make it as easy as possible for the influence target to take that most essential step?

Let's revisit some of the request examples in Table 5.2 and consider how to change the effort dynamics to increase the likelihood of gaining compliance.

Example 1: Request for a reference letter

Presumably, the requester and receiver know one other and the requester expects that the receiver has a positive impression of him or her. The strength of affiliation the receiver feels will certainly affect how much effort the receiver is willing to make. However, writing the request probably took around one minute. To comply with this request, the receiver would need to:

- Access the link and identify what is required;
- Recall information about this particular person (who might be one of many to the receiver);
- Set aside time away from his/her own work priorities;
- Compose and format the text of the letter;
- Identify where to send the letter.

Moreover, the topic does not have high relevance to the receiver because it is very unlikely that the receiver's current needs involve providing other people with references. Hence, on average across

TABLE 5.3: Making it as easy as possible (reference letter request)

What is the least effort/most essential step that I need from the influence target?	Influence target to sign his or her name on an appropriate reference letter and submit it on behalf of the candidate.
How can I make it as easy as possible to take that most essential step?	• Draft and format the reference letter, ensuring it meets the requirements found in the link; • Invite receiver to edit the letter as he/she sees fit; • Indicate where the letter should be signed; • Provide the link or address to which the finished letter should be sent; • Review your request message using Table 5.1 to make it as easy as possible to read – and ensure it is very polite!

the population, there will be many unsuccessful requests of this kind made to people who do not consider it a priority to help. Instead of pleading extra hard – or resending the email over again (annoying!), Table 5.3 uses the two questions above to substantially reduce how much work the receiver must do.

According to the new approach, the requester is required to take on the bulk of the effort. That is entirely appropriate, because it is the requester who wants the outcome to happen. The effort required from the receiver is distilled down to the bare minimum, so it is now more likely that he or she will be willing to comply.

To take an example from the other end of Table 5.2, let's also apply this approach to the request sent through by a person asking for advice on how to prepare for an event.

Example 2: Request for advice on preparing an event

Once again, the writing of this request probably took around one minute. To comply with this request, the receiver would need to:

- Re-focus attention on the topic of event preparation;
- Analyze their past experience to identify their top tips;
- Make a guess regarding what might help the person (note that the requester has provided no details, either of what steps they have taken already or what type of event it is);
- Write all of this into the reply message.

Again, Table 5.4 uses the same two questions to identify how to substantially reduce the effort required by the receiver.

In either case (Tables 5.3 or 5.4), there is no guarantee that the receiver will comply. However, by significantly reducing the effort required to respond, the requester can improve the likelihood that the person will take some action. It is much easier to look at a list of four steps and identify whether or not there might be one crucial step missing than it is to generate your own list of tips and suggestions from scratch. On top, imagine how annoyed the receiver would be if the requester replied saying 'thank you, but I thought of these steps already'.

TABLE 5.4: Making it as easy as possible (request for advice)

What is the least effort/most essential step that I need from the influence target?	In essence, the requester wants to know if there is one major thing he or she has forgotten, or one overall recommendation that may improve their event.
How can I make it as easy as possible to take that most essential step?	• Write a clear, simple list of the main steps you have taken to prepare for the event. Something like four or five bullet points of no more than two sentences in length each is about right; • Ask the receiver to review the list and add the most important thing they believe is missing; • Review your request message using Table 5.1 to make it as easy as possible to read.

Following these two examples, review again the effort dynamics of the remaining requests in Table 5.2.* Probably you will find that the dynamics are even more extreme than you considered the first time around. For example, in number 2 (position enquiry), there is a ridiculously low likelihood that the receiver of this request will expend the high degree of time and effort required to meet with an unknown person simply to help them understand more about the company. Perhaps if 10,000 people sent a request such as this, one of them might secure a meeting – in the same way that chimpanzees hitting a keyboard might eventually type a proper sentence. This requester is asking for far too much effort from a person who does not know them and the only effort that person has bothered to make for themselves is typing a few sentences and finding an email address. In order to increase his or her chances of success, the requester needs to completely rethink what they are trying to achieve and how they can match any aspect of what they seek with something that involves such little effort the receiver just might comply. If the requester is unable to find a match between what they want the other to do, and what that person is likely to do, then they will be better off conserving their own energy by refraining from making such requests in the first place.

In contrast, it might be easier to significantly improve your chances of success in example 5 (meeting request). First, if the requester has expertise in the topic of the client meeting, then some aspect of the meeting might indeed be relevant or useful to the receiver's own deliverables or needs. Investigate that. If the topic clearly has relevance to the receiver, you might increase their willingness to at least think about the request – or at very least, read the rest of the email. How else can you reduce the effort required by your influence target? Perhaps you can plan the meeting specifically around their availability and start the meeting by addressing the topic for which you most need them. This reduces the effort they must make to attend the meeting because they are free to leave after the first topic.

---

* To view our answers to this exercise and compare your own, go to dramandanimonpeters. com

Even when asking another person about their availability for a meeting, your question can require more or less effort from the other person. Asking a very open question such as 'when would you be available?' in fact requires more mental effort than providing some very simple guidance such as 'would it suit you better to hold the meeting this week or next week?' Although the person may choose a different time altogether, providing a simple option or two makes the mental processing easier than asking a fully open question. However, don't bombard the receiver with options to choose from because reading through a lot of questions is also work.

How to remember and apply the Principle of Effort

Given that you are also more likely to do things that are easy, you might be looking for the simplest way to remember to apply Principle Five. Here is a statement with high information content and a low number of words: *Make it as easy as possible for people to do what you want them to do.* Or alternatively:

'You will be more influential if you ask someone to push a button rather than push a boulder'

What is the 'button pushing' version of what you want the other person to do? In general, the better the fit between the key thing you request and the minimal effort the receiver is willing to spend, the higher your chances of achieving the outcome you seek.

BETTER THAN YESTERDAY: OVERCOMING PROCRASTINATION USING THE PRINCIPLE OF EFFORT

You may recall from Principle Two (*Social Imitation*) that one of the reasons we tend to adopt the choices of people around us is that it makes decisions easier. Decision fatigue is indeed a good illustration of the principle of effort: it takes effort to make decisions and so one way to reduce this effort is to do what others have done. Similarly, given the extent to which our brains are programmed to avoid effort, it is not surprising that we procrastinate working on demanding or lengthy tasks that require a lot of mental processing.

If you have ever found yourself putting off difficult but nonetheless necessary work, I hope it is clear by now that there is nothing particularly 'wrong' with you, despite the fact that this procrastination is not particularly helpful. To overcome it, there are a number of simple methodologies that can help you manage the effort involved in sustained concentration so that you will find it easier to make a start on the work needed. One such technique is the Pomodoro Technique, in which the worker uses a timing device to commit to spending just 25 minutes at a time against a difficult task.[24] After 25 minutes of dedicated concentration or effort, the worker is then required to spend five minutes engaged in very low effort activities, such as walking around the room or breathing exercises. This '25 minutes on, five minutes off' pattern can be repeated up to three times, but after four complete revolutions the participant should take a longer break. Just like breaking a long journey into several smaller steps, the Pomodoro Technique is one of several methods that makes effort seem less daunting by packaging it into smaller parcels of work.

ILLUSTRATION OF PRINCIPLE FIVE (*EFFORT*) FIGURE 5

FIGURE 5: Pushing a button is easy. Pushing a boulder uphill is difficult. Which one are you asking people to do for you?

Key takeaways

- Humans display a high propensity to avoid mental and physical effort until they are required to exert it for something they need or want.

- When we make requests of others, our default approach focuses on what we want from them instead of what they are willing to do.

- Make it as easy as possible for people to do what you want them to do. In other words, you will be more influential if you ask someone to push a button rather than a boulder.

- When we significantly reduce the effort involved in complying with requests, we dramatically increase our chances of successfully influencing others.

Principle Six

Reasoning (How to Do It Better)

Executive summary

The single most frequently used tactic to influence other people at work is reasoning – that is, providing the other person with good reasons why they should do what you are asking of them. We default to this approach because it is reflexive for us; when we want something, it is pretty easy to think of the reasons we want it. However, when you examine how this plays out across the thousands of requests people make of each other at work, the research indicates that our most common approach to influencing others is far less effective than we believe it to be. In this chapter you will discover ways to develop your ability to generate reasons that are more influential than the average approach. You will also learn how to combine some of the principles from previous chapters to further increase your influencing power.

CAN YOU GET AHEAD IN A QUEUE?

If you found yourself at the end of a queue to photocopy a short document, what would you say to persuade people ahead of you to let you go through? Of course, your first question might be why on earth would you need a photocopier – and my answer would be because the crucial psychology experiment at the foundation of this chapter was conducted in 1978. While the setting of that experiment is outdated, the principle we will examine is invaluable, newly discovered, and still highly effective. Technology has evolved enormously since 1978, but the human brain, not so much.

In class at business school, I pose this scenario to my students, asking them how they would persuade a person already in the queue to let them make five copies first.

The most common statement generated involves explaining to those in the queue that you are under significant pressure because your manager needs these copies urgently and you have to get back to meet a deadline. Some answers even go on to explain that your job is at stake, or to include similarly disastrous outcomes that might befall the speaker, should he or she not return immediately with the required copies. The second most common response involves negotiating with the person in the queue, or offering an incentive, or even attempting to take the person's details to reciprocate with a valuable favour or gift at a later date.

But in experiments, what happens? When Harvard Social Psychologist Ellen Langer and her colleagues conducted this experiment by sending students out to photocopiers around the community, they started with a baseline request 'Excuse me, I have five pages. May I use the copy machine?'[1] They found that 60 per cent of people approached in this way complied, demonstrating that simply asking was all that was required to get ahead and all that elaborate negotiating and pleading was completely unnecessary. Only one additional ingredient was required to increase compliance from 60 per cent all the way up to 93 per cent: the researchers added a reason to the statement request. Yet the reason that had this effect had nothing to do with deadlines or impending disasters. Now the requesters simply said 'Excuse me, I have five pages. May I use the copy machine **because I have to make copies**'. Indeed, there was no significant difference in the compliance produced between this statement and a third condition in which the request ended with the reason '**because I am in a rush**'.

If the people standing in front of you in the queue (the influence targets) needed a reason to comply with your request, one would think 'because I have to make copies' is a pretty poor one. Presumably, everyone queueing at a photocopier is there to make copies. My question to you is, what is happening in the minds of the influence target, if this nonsensical request produces such high compliance rates?

We can find a clue to the process by changing a variable and running the experiment again. In the second rendition of the experiment, the confederates had 20 pages to copy. This is four times as many pages as in the first rendition. Hence, the effort being requested of the target at the photocopier was higher because he or she would be inconvenienced for much longer. Under this new condition, overall compliance dropped dramatically. The request 'Excuse me, I have 20 pages. May I use the copy machine?' was met with just 24 per cent compliance. Nonetheless this result demonstrates that simply asking for help will sometimes lead to the outcome you seek and also that people can be nicer than you might expect them to be (or at least they were in 1978).

However, this time around, a statement modelled on the previously successful approach – 'Excuse me, I have 20 pages. May I use the copy machine **because I have to make copies**' – was no more effective than simply asking to go ahead. In other words, when the cost to the influence target was higher, the addition of the (rather ridiculous) reason 'I have to make copies' resulted in the same 24 per cent success rate, indicating that this reason added nothing to the statement's influencing power. Under the third condition, when the reason given was changed to 'because I am in a rush', compliance increased significantly from the first and second examples, now reaching 42 per cent. Note that compliance was nonetheless lower under all of these request conditions when the cost to the target was relatively high.

What does this tell us about the thought processes of the influence target and thus about the science of influence? When comparing the results, set out in Table 6.1, we can draw the following conclusions:

TABLE 6.1: Compliance achieved relative to 1) effort involved in request and 2) presence of reason

Request	Percentage of targets who complied	
	Five copies	20 copies
Excuse me, I have x pages. May I use the copy machine?	60 per cent	24 per cent
Excuse me, I have x pages. May I use the copy machine because I have to make copies?	93 per cent	24 per cent
Excuse me, I have x pages. May I use the copy machine because I am in a rush?	94 per cent	42 per cent

(Adapted from Langer et al.[1])

1. **Effort**: When the request has a small cost for the target it is much easier to gain compliance than when the request has a high cost. This is precisely what we would expect on the basis of Principle Five (*Effort*).

2. **Importance of Reason**: The higher the effort that would be required for compliance, the more the receiver will scrutinize the reason provided to determine whether or not that reason is sufficient grounds for acting. Conversely, when the effort required is low, the receiver appears to be positively influenced by the presence of any reason, no matter how unimportant or even meaningless.

GIVE ME A REASON

This second observation regarding the importance of the reason is easy to observe in daily life. Back when I used to interview supermarket shoppers about their choice of one shampoo brand over another, people would often cite the '10 per cent off' label on the shelf as the reason they chose that particular item. This seems highly logical until you follow up with the question 'what is the price of this item?' and find that those same shoppers do not know the price. As per the discussion of 'comparison sets' in Principle

Four (*Value Framing*), once a shopper has defined a comparison set of two or three brands they perceive as largely equivalent, they will look for any reason to choose one over the other. As a result, the presence of any apparent reason to drive the choice one way can be enough to seal the deal – even when that reason is not very good. If you don't know the price of the two brands in the first place, it is safe to say that 10 per cent off the cost of one of them is not a very good reason.

ARE PEOPLE GOOD AT USING REASONS TO INFLUENCE OTHERS?

Not really. As discussed already in Chapter Five, the tactics with which we attempt to influence people at work demonstrate that we have a poor operational understanding of the effectiveness of different approaches in the workplace. Rational persuasion – using logical reasoning in an attempt to persuade another to comply – is one of the most frequently used approaches[2,3,4], probably because it requires the least amount of psychological effort to generate.[5] While rational persuasion is actually among the more effective of the *naturally occurring* influence tactics used by employees, it still has a generally low correlation with achieving the outcome that person is seeking. In Lee et al.'s meta-analysis of 49 studies, covering the workplace behaviour of almost 9,000 people, the correlation coefficient was estimated to be 0.35, which indicates that rational persuasion influencers are successful about 12 per cent of the time.[3]

Why we are not particularly good at generating reasons that influence others

1. **We don't just ask:** Studies demonstrate that we underestimate the effectiveness of simply asking for help.[6,7] Further, employees might refrain from asking for help because of embarrassment, especially in individualistic cultures (such as North America), compared to collectivist cultures (such as China).[8] As seen in Langer's photocopier

experiment above, simply asking for help can achieve the
outcome we seek, especially if the cost to the target is low.

2. **We are wrong about what will be effective**: Even when
very clever people take the time to compose reasons that
they expect to be highly persuasive, they are often wrong
in their expectation of what will work. Major public
health campaigns attempting to use rational persuasion
to influence people to stop smoking, quit alcohol
abuse, or avoid teenage pregnancy have frequently been
found to be completely ineffective in changing people's
behaviour in any measurable way.[9] Similarly, research
on energy consumption in the UK found that more
than two-thirds of consumers could not be persuaded to
adopt efficiency measures because of logical reasons such
as reducing usage or saving money. Instead, they were
more likely to be influenced if they knew the efficiency
measures could be installed without causing them any
inconvenience.[10]

3. **We think more is better**: We believe that the greater the
number of logical reasons we add to our arguments, the
more convincing we will be. In fact, the opposite has been
shown to be true. One study of over 1,000 American
consumers found that their willingness to enrol in an
energy savings programme decreased when two logical
reasons were used in place of one.[11] Another study of
human resources managers in Quebec, Canada, found
that those who attempted to strengthen their logical
arguments by including additional data and reasons
were actually less influential than colleagues who did
not.[12] Both Falbe and Yukl's[13] and Lee et al.'s[3] overview
of published studies found that the average effectiveness
of rational persuasion drops when would-be influencers
combine their reasons. In fact, thanks to a phenomenon
called the 'dilution effect', providing additional content in
your message can divert people's attention away from the
very information that might otherwise be persuasive.[14]

More factors that undermine the effectiveness of our logical reasons

People's feelings affect how they interpret information

Psychologists have known for many years that our evaluation of information is significantly affected by how we are feeling at the time. In one study, researchers used news stories about either happy or sad events to invoke those same emotions in their study participants.[15] People in a negative mood rated themselves as more likely to fall victim to a fatal accident (e.g., struck by lightning) compared with those in a positive mood, although they had the same information about the likelihood of the event. Similarly, students who were manipulated to be in a mild good mood (e.g., money was left on the chair they were asked to sit on) rated ambiguous scenes as positive, while those put in a mild bad mood (e.g., received a discouraging message) rated the same scenes as negative.[16] In fact, German and Dutch researchers have identified a wide range of emotional reactions and feelings that affect how we evaluate data and information. These include: 1) feelings inspired by the topic itself; 2) incidental feelings inspired by stimuli other than the topic; 3) feelings about the information itself, such as whether the information is familiar or fits with things already believed.[17]

Your perceived expertise matters

Unless you are perceived by those you are attempting to influence as someone with authority in the subject, your logical reasons may be dismissed subconsciously by the listener. A recent study in Austria found that safety engineers were better able to influence management decisions using rational persuasion tactics when they were perceived as having high expert status as engineers.[18] Undergraduate students at the University of Hong Kong shopping online for a digital camera were influenced by the rational arguments of virtual agents when the avatar giving advice was considered to have a professional appearance.[19] In other words, the influencing power of a logical reason is moderated by the speaker's perceived status and expertise on the topic.

The reasons we use are not very good ones

When we believe that a specific action needs to be taken, the reasons that are easiest to think of are those that matter most to us. However, reasons that matter to us do not necessarily matter to the influence target. Consider your own experience in the workplace. It is likely you can think of times you've been asked to complete a task because the requester 'really, really needs it', or because the author of an email 'is facing a tight deadline'. Do you honestly care about their needs or their deadlines? Quite possibly not at all, unless the requester themselves has some particular significance for you, such as your boss or close friend.

In general, the approach we take to any kind of problem solving (including influencing) tends to be reflexive unless we are specifically directed to be creative.[20] Many of our attempts at using reasons to influence others will also be reflexive, hence the *'because I really need it'* approach to influencing. When someone does pause in advance to plan an influencing strategy – just as my Executive MBA students are asked to do in the photocopier exercise – they devise statements that incorporate an overwhelming barrage of reasons why the person ahead should permit them to jump the queue. However, we now know that using many reasons is often less effective than using just

TABLE 6.2: Six factors that undermine logical reasons

Your logical reasons and supporting data are affected by many factors. Typically, people do not consider these factors when generating reasons intended to influence others.

1	The target's current emotional state (positive or negative)
2	The influence target's feelings about the topic, the context, or the messenger
3	The extent to which your reasons or information fits with things the influence target already believes
4	The influence target's perception of your expertise or status in the subject
5	The importance of the reason to the target
6	Using a message packed full of many reasons or other diluting information

one important reason – and that using multiple reasons that are of little consequence to the influence target is an even bigger waste of energy. In summary, the use of logical reasoning as a means to influence people and outcomes is undermined by many factors, which are presented together in Table 6.2.

PLANNING TO INFLUENCE PEOPLE AND OUTCOMES USING PRINCIPLE SIX

Start by choosing a real-life practice scenario

In order to increase your ability to generate reasons with stronger than average influencing power, you will need to practise. A good starting point is to choose a real-life situation you can use as a practice exercise. To begin with, this should be something that does not carry high consequences if it does not work out. Even the best strategy does not pay out every single time and for now it is more important that you focus on developing your ability in the technique, whether or not you achieve immediate success. In other words, you might find that you don't win the influencing game during your first attempts, but if you develop your capability, it will eventually pay out on an occasion that does matter. Hence, start with something relatively harmless and familiar, such as influencing what your household will have for dinner tomorrow night or asking a friend to pick you up on the way to a meeting.

A THREE-STEP APPROACH TO GENERATE BETTER REASONS

When you follow the three-step process below, be strict in sticking to the recommendations. For example, **you may not use** non-technique approaches like offering to give everyone money if they eat vegetables or promising to do the dishes for a week. These kinds of wild and lavish arguments might work as a one-off on your flatmate, but they do not translate into effective long-term workplace tactics. The goal at this stage is to learn the methodology rather than to achieve the desired outcome – work on being able to follow the process.

Step 1: Focus on benefits, not information

We respond more strongly to the perception of rewards and benefits than to rational and logical arguments. Emotional reactions play a greater role in driving our behaviour than rational decisions. In essence, the brain learns by associating actions or decisions with the expectation of reward or punishment.

The science backs this up. Health scientist Valerie Curtis suggests that you can better influence people to exercise if you suggest it will make them more attractive (reward-oriented reason), compared to explaining how it will make them healthier (generic reason).[9] Curtis was part of a team that ran a spectacularly successful public health campaign aiming to influence rural mothers in Ghana to wash their hands using soap. The team undertook significant qualitative research to uncover what mattered to their target group and to identify a motivation they would find rewarding. When they found the most influential reason for washing your hands with soap (providing better care for your children), they created a campaign focused on this reason alone – and refrained from listing further reasons that might distract the audience. As a result, the proportion of rural mothers engaging in the desired behaviour increased from 2 per cent to 71 per cent.[21] In a recent study of the factors that cause people to share video content on social media, Japanese and Australian neuroscientists found they could predict what content would go viral by measuring a neural response in the brains of people watching.[22] When their brains lit up in a region that represents an expectation of social approval, people were likely to share the video. In contrast, people's spoken intention to share a video among their friends did not predict whether or not they would actually go on to do so. Once again, we find that our conscious explanation of what influences us is not very accurate.

For step one, list all the possible reward-oriented benefits that might accrue to someone who complies with the request in your practice example. Don't cut the list short at this stage: make it as long as you can. In Table 6.3 you will find examples of generic reasons compared to reward-oriented benefits. This is just for illustration purposes. Your list should include only reward-oriented benefits because that's what you should be using.

TABLE 6.3: Examples of reward-oriented benefits compared to generic 'good reasons' for two practice scenarios

Desired behaviour: Picking me up on the way to (meeting, party, cinema)

Reward-oriented benefits	Generic reasons
I have important information we need to discuss	We can split the cost of the trip
I want to tell you about a (job, opportunity or potential date) that would be perfect for you	It is barely out of your way
I baked breakfast muffins that smell amazing	I will be ready exactly on time
Arriving at the event with a friend will make you look popular	It is fewer kilometres to drive if you take this route
You can rehearse your speech with me before the meeting, so you do a great job in front of the boss	Car-pooling is better for the environment

Desired behaviour: Participating in a new work project

Reward-oriented benefits	Generic reasons
This project will help you meet one of your targets this quarter	This will help the team
This project will show you are better than your predecessor	This will help us meet a deadline
You will be the only person at your level taking part in such an important project	This will reduce costs/increase sales
This opportunity will demonstrate you are ready for higher leadership	This will be good for the brand/ company
Senior management named you as the expert for this team	This is important for senior management

Step 2: Personalize the benefits to the target (without being creepy)

Review your list of reward-oriented benefits and consider how you could tailor this better to the specific person concerned. Working on your chosen practice example, consider his or her interests, needs, concerns, socializing preferences and what they do for fun. What does this tell you about the rewards that would matter to them? Also, consider the language that person might use to express the benefit, because the more familiar the idea sounds, the more influential it will be.

When you plan influence attempts for the workplace, you should also consider the person's role, department, or company. Do you know anything about their specific objectives? Or about the values or objectives of the team within which they work? Online searches and LinkedIn can be helpful here if the person has a digital presence. On one occasion I represented a retail distribution client in Kuwait to a big brand name company from which my client hoped to win distribution rights for the country. The meeting in Kuwait City was to be attended by the CEO, who – very fortunately for me – had been involved in many public speaking events and social outreach initiatives recently. After gaining an understanding of his interests, I was able to subtly weave some of those values and some of that language into the opening few minutes of my presentation. The meeting was a success and I felt extremely well prepared going into it.

If there is someone at work you want to influence in the future, consider getting to know them now, ahead of time, so you have knowledge of what interests them before you need it. The best approach is to ask questions that prompt the person to talk about what motivates them and matters to them. Listen to both the content and the terminology. Subtlety is crucial in this endeavour. You must not create the impression you are stalking them, sucking up to them, prying or being overly familiar, as any of these will incite suspicion: you are looking just for information they will easily divulge. Equally important – you must not ever directly refer to 'what they have told you' or repeat it back to them. If you do this, you are drawing attention to the fact that you planned in advance to influence them using their own words. That could create resistance, or produce a sense of betrayal, and will almost certainly brand you as creepy.

Step 3: Plan what, when and where to make the influence attempt
Steps 1 and 2 have enabled you to address several of the undermining factors listed in Table 6.2. In order to increase your chances of success further still, the final step is to select your best reward-oriented reason and decide when and where to make the influence attempt with your target person.

If you are going to be speaking to the person, or calling them, consider what you know about when they are likely to be in the best mood and what is the best setting for making your request. If you are going to be emailing them, consider how the subject line of your email might affect their attention and how they might feel about opening that email. Consider also that people typically direct their attention to their emails first thing in the morning: it might pay to send the message very early, so it appears at the top of their inbox and gets their attention. When delivering your message do not succumb to the temptation of piling in more reasons or more information, because that is unlikely to help.

Finally, recognize that influencing with reasons – just as influencing with any of these principles – is a capability you will improve on, if you work at it. You won't get the outcome you seek every single time, but there is a lot you can do to tip things in your favour.

THE RESISTANCE RATIO: A SIMPLE CONCEPTUAL MODEL FOR INCREASING YOUR INFLUENCE AT WORK

In reviewing our conclusions from Langer's photocopier experiment, we can identify a simple model for conceptualizing how to increase your influencing power, or rather **reduce the resistance of the person you wish to influence**.

Langer's findings suggest that the likelihood an influence target complies with a request is determined by the relationship between the cost of complying with that request (e.g., effort or inconvenience) and the importance of the reason given for the request. We will call this relationship the ***Resistance Ratio*** in which the cost of the request is divided by the importance of the reason. The smaller the resulting value, the lower the target's barrier to helping you. Of course, the calculation is figurative rather than literal.

Hence, we can express the Resistance Ratio as:

$$\frac{Cost\ of\ Request}{Importance\ of\ Reason}$$

Where the smaller the resulting value, the lower the resistance to complying with your request, hence the higher your likelihood of success.

To demonstrate the model's effectiveness, let's apply it to Langer et al.'s results.

Under the '5-page' condition:

$$\frac{Cost\ is\ low}{Importance\ of\ reason\ is\ low}$$

Output value: The overall value remains low (aka barrier is low)
    Result: Relatively high compliance

Under the '20-page' condition:

$$\frac{Cost\ is\ high}{Importance\ of\ reason\ is\ low}$$

Output value: The overall value remains high (aka barrier is high)
    Result: Relatively low compliance, with small improvement when the value of the reason increased

Let us consider another demonstration of this model: you receive an email from a restaurant you visited a week ago, asking you to complete a feedback survey to help them improve. You open the survey to discover it is 15 pages of detailed questions. Chances are, you will close the survey – and indeed surveys of this type generally receive a low response rate. Here the cost is high (perhaps 30 minutes of your time), and the importance is negligible: you don't know the people and you are unlikely to care much about their request for feedback. Hence, the Resistance Ratio is even higher than that in the '20-page' condition: The cost is very high, and the importance of the reason is very low.

An example in the opposite direction occurs when children pester their parents to add a small treat to the total shopping basket at a queue in a supermarket checkout. A study of 135 South African families with children found that the kids were veritable masterminds of influence.[23] The children in this study were extremely adept at playing on their parents' emotions, leveraging the high importance of the reason for buying a treat. As any parent will tell you, providing happiness to your child (or stopping them from making a scene) is a very important reason. Further, when you have just completed a grocery run, the cost of one additional chocolate bar seems very small in comparison with the cost of the total bill.* As a result, the cost of the request is low and the importance is very high, so we can use the Resistance Ratio to predict that this approach has a strong likelihood of success – exactly as the researchers discovered.

THE RESISTANCE RATIO COMBINES KNOWLEDGE FROM PRINCIPLES THREE, FIVE AND SIX

In addition to the techniques for increasing the importance of your reasons provided in this chapter, you can also leverage the skills you have learned from other principles in this book. For example:

Principle Three (*Affiliation*): The stronger your affiliation with the influence target, the greater the emotional attachment the

---

* This is Principle Four (*Value Framing*) at work

target will feel for you, hence the higher the importance of your reason. As detailed in Principle Three (*Affiliation*), we are more likely to agree to requests from people we like (or people with the same name!).

Principle Five (*Effort*): As detailed in Principle Five (*Effort*) people are most likely to conserve physical and mental effort unless they have a good reason for expending it. We noted that people in the workplace often make substantial requests of others who have low inclination to exert effort for the reasons provided in the message. The example above in which a restaurant owner you do not know asks you to complete a 15-page survey from a restaurant is another example of that same effort dynamic.

Thus, the Resistance Ratio provides a simple conceptual approach to planning your influence attempt. Leverage Principle Five to consider how to identify the precise, minimum degree of effort you truly need from your influence target to reduce the cost of the request. Leverage Principle Three to consider how to highlight your affiliation with the target to increase the importance of the reason. Leverage Principle Six to develop reasons that have more influencing power than the average.

Finally, Principle One (*Status*) might offer an additional route to increasing the importance of your reason. As per Table 6.2, the greater your expertise or the more senior you are, the more effective your logical reasons might be. Indeed, Lee et al.'s[3] overview of influence tactics that commonly occur in the workplace found that rational persuasion was more likely to achieve the desired outcome when the influence occurred from a senior person to a more junior person. When the influence attempt occurred from a junior person to a more senior person, the use of logical reasoning was much less effective than the standard 12 per cent. The Resistance Ratio predicts a change in effectiveness as the importance of the reason changes.

If you feel discouraged because the average junior person has a hard time influencing the average senior person, there is no need for you to despair. None of the people included in Lee et al.'s study had the benefit of being able to read this book. In contrast, you are well equipped to perform better than average!

BETTER THAN YESTERDAY: USING THIS KNOWLEDGE TO IMPROVE EMOTIONAL HEALTH

The relationship between how you feel and how you interpret information is stronger than you might think. Recall that seemingly innocuous incidents such as finding money on a chair or receiving a discouraging message can colour your perception to a significant and measurable extent. When your interpretation of an interaction or a piece of news is negative, you won't attribute this negativity to external factors such as a sad story you just heard on the radio, even though a very recent but unconnected event might be the reason you feel bad.

The next time you find yourself feeling down about your day, pessimistic about a company announcement, or discouraged about a piece of work, give yourself a small break from the situation to change your perspective. Activities that can prompt you into a better mood include going for a brisk walk outdoors, watching a 20-minute episode of a comedy series, or making a call to someone who makes you laugh. After gaining a little distance from the situation, and nudging your mood with one of these activities, reassess the reason you had for being pessimistic. Do you notice any change in perception?

ILLUSTRATION OF PRINCIPLE SIX
(*REASONING*) FIGURE 6

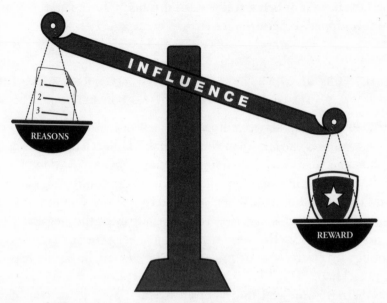

FIGURE 6: We tend to give people logical reasons. They are far more influenced by rewards.

Key takeaways

- Influence attempts in which people use reasons as a method of persuasion are very common, but not particularly effective.

- The reasons people use in influence attempts are often ineffective because they reflexively generate reasons that matter to themselves.

- In fact, people are more influenced by the perception of rewards and benefits than by information-based generic reasons.

- The effectiveness of reasons used in influence attempts is also impacted by how the receiver feels at the time, whether the information feels likely or familiar, and the perceived expertise of the messenger. Moreover, while it might be tempting to think that adding lots of reasons will increase your influencing power, studies suggest you will be more effective by limiting your message to one important, benefit-based reason.

- The more you know about the target of your influence attempt including their interests, needs, targets, role, and organization, the better placed you will be to identify reasons that matter to him or her. However, don't directly refer to this knowledge in your influence attempt or the person with whom you have been building a relationship may feel betrayed (or even stalked!).

- A valuable conceptual model for reducing another's barrier to complying with your request is to minimize the cost or effort involved in executing your request and to maximize the importance of the reason for compliance. The lower this overall ratio, the lower their barrier to action, thus the higher your influence power.

- You can also apply skills you have developed in studying earlier principles – such as Principles Three and Five – to the conceptual model outlined in this chapter.

Principle Seven

Inertia (Be Like Water)

Executive summary

Imagine human behaviour occurs with a force of inertia; that is a force that keeps an object in motion or continuing along a set path. Like physical inertia, this behavioural inertia propels people to behave in a predictable manner in response to various social and environmental stimuli. As a result, it can be hard for individuals to put the brakes on a behavioural sequence or alter its course once it has begun. Reactions are performed as if automatic, or at least without much conscious awareness. The behavioural pattern that is driven through inertia might be almost species-wide, common to members of a particular group, or specific to an individual. With knowledge and practice, you can learn to identify the chain of behaviours most likely to occur then, instead of fighting that inertia, use the flow of activity to your advantage. Given what is most likely to happen, what is your best move? How can you be prepared and decisive at the key moments when others will be unprepared and indecisive?

BE LIKE WATER

Wing Chun is a form of Chinese Kung Fu that promotes harnessing an opponent's strength and inertia instead of resisting or retaliating with force.[1] The philosophy involves using another's movement and energy to your advantage, much like sailing involves harnessing – instead of fighting – the energy of the wind and waves. The influential martial artist Bruce Lee originally trained in Wing Chun. He is credited with saying 'Be like water making its way through cracks. Do not be assertive, but adjust to the object, and you shall find a way around or through it'.[2] Lee would have intuitively understood Principle Seven. In this chapter, you will learn to identify recurring behavioural patterns in professional settings and use, rather than resist, those patterns to your advantage in influencing attempts.

Back in Chapter Five (*Effort*), we learned that human brains act as if programmed to seek out the easiest, least effort means to achieve a given end. Bearing in mind that people are most likely to do whatever comes easiest to them, I asked you to consider what the target of your influence attempt is most likely to do under a given set of conditions. In Chapter Seven, we will further explore the concept of what people are most likely to do. There are many social and environmental stimuli that elicit predictable behavioural patterns in others. When you perceive and even search for these patterns you can adjust to them and harness them – so that you, too, can be like water.

BEHAVIOURAL INERTIA EXPLAINED

As a phenomenon studied in physics, inertia is the force that acts to keep an object in its current state of motion. This force is readily observed when you are driving forward in a car then suddenly hit the brakes: your body will fall forward as you continue to move in the same direction until stopped by your seatbelt (hopefully). That 'falling forward' is inertia in action.

Now imagine that people's behaviour also comes with a force of inertia underneath it. Visualize this inertia as propelling them to behave, or continue behaving, according to an expected pattern. Both as a species and as individuals, we have some strong and relatively predictable behavioural patterns such that a given situation can elicit an expected response. Further, once we begin a behavioural sequence, we find it hard to stop midway through a series of actions that our brains expect us to execute.

Behavioural inertia makes it easy for us to perform activities linked in a routine without much conscious effort (e.g., preparing your morning coffee in auto-mode). It can also leave us shocked and immobilized when circumstances prevent us from continuing as expected (e.g., discovering a hole in your suit pants and choosing whether to continue to the meeting or head back home). Being forced to stop a behavioural pattern when we have become accustomed to performing it is frustrating, at the very least. More serious consequences of behavioural inertia occur when dramatic changes in the workplace leave people unable to perform their expected daily routines.[3] During 2020, when the global pandemic prevented people from going about their regular lives as expected, anxiety levels increased across the population at large.[4]

Although you may not be used to thinking about it, many of our behaviours do not occur independently, but instead are elicited within a specific context and in response to a given stimulus or set of stimuli. The contextual stimuli that elicit your behaviour might be an object (like a refrigerator door), people (such as a roommate you want to avoid), other people's recurring behaviour (your parent yelling at you again) or a culturally established expectation (you know you're not supposed to speak when you're in a library). Your behaviour might involve just one action (yelling back at your parent) or it could involve a sequence of behaviours that have become tied together (e.g., open the refrigerator door, look carefully at all of the contents, cut a tiny sliver off your roommate's food, then finish chewing and swallowing while the door is still open to conceal your action).

WHERE CAN I SEE BEHAVIOURAL INERTIA IN ACTION?

My first observations of behavioural inertia occurred while working as a waitress in Adelaide, South Australia, around the time that I first became interested in studying psychology. I noticed over and over again that different customers would make the same jokes in the same situation. A joke made by a customer in response to a simple question (e.g., 'Would you like anything else?' 'Yes please, $1000!') might come from a young man in a cycling outfit or a grandmother treating her grandkids. Irrespective of their apparent differences, they responded in the same way to the same stimuli. Since those days, I have observed many examples of diverse people behaving in the same manner in response to the same stimuli. For example, MBA students from countries across the world tend not to read prescribed papers over five pages in length and unprepared or flustered speakers begin their presentations with a predictably stream-of-consciousness series of statements.

Specific behavioural sequences are sometimes so common across members of a species that they seem to affect almost every member, in which case science might label them as 'innate' or 'genetically hardwired'.[5] For example, we can expect that almost any person in the world would turn to look at someone who is staring at them. People also turn to look at an object that many other people are already looking at. These predictable, species-wide reactions have been used by advertising researchers, who learned that consumers are more likely to look at products when a human face in the advertisement is also looking at that product.[6,7]

Another instance of behavioural inertia occurs when a person implements a sequence of actions that they recognize is expected of them in a specific setting. Think about the routine activities expected of you when you walk into a hotel, enter a lift, or arrive at a birthday party. What is the appropriate thing to do first in this situation? What would be considered rude? Your underlying understanding of what actions should be taken in a given situation is known as a 'behavioural script'.[8] A common understanding of behavioural scripts can be shared among members of an organization[9] as well as members of a pre-school.[10] Scripts are learned within cultural and social contexts – such as families, companies and countries – because we consciously or subconsciously seek out an understanding of how to behave appropriately according to the situation. The inertia of a behavioural script is evident when a colleague asks, 'How are you?' and you reply 'Fine, thanks. How are you?' pretty much without pause or thinking, even when you have no interest in receiving an honest answer.

Behavioural inertia is also observed when an individual executes a series of behaviours that he or she has learned to perform together in a specific order in a specific context. The scientific term for this is 'behaviour chain'.[11,12] Chains are thought to occur because a person has learned that performing those behaviours together produces a valuable benefit – such as saving on time or effort. The more often a person performs the same chain, the more likely it is to become a habit that occurs automatically.[13] Chains are generally learned by individuals but can be similar between people (e.g., many of us have a routine chain of behaviours that start with picking up the toothpaste and end with having clean teeth). A behaviour chain might also involve coming home from work, opening the fridge, getting a drink, then sitting in front of the TV, or progressing from leaving your bed to getting into your car without having to think much about what to do in-between. The same sequence learned so that you can save brain power on a weekday can also lead you to drive to the office on a Saturday when you were intending to go somewhere else.

Overall, the most important insight about behavioural inertia is that people's standard behaviour in a common situation can be relatively predictable and you can use that predictability to help you achieve the outcome you seek. If you are a student or professor of behavioural sciences, you may recognize that our description of behavioural inertia groups together a wide variety of phenomena that scientists who develop theory might prefer to keep separated. That does not matter for our purposes, because grouping these phenomena together enables us to respond to them as a category. Further, whatever the reason the inertia exists, we are not going to try to change it. Instead, we are going to use the concept of behavioural inertia to predict the most likely behaviour of people in a given situation and then leverage the opportunities that this foresight creates to exert influence on people and outcomes.

LEARN TO IDENTIFY INERTIA AT WORK: WHAT DO PEOPLE DO NEXT?

When a stranger in a train station says you have a stain on your clothes and points to your chest, the pickpocket knows you will be distracted for the few seconds needed to take your purse or your wallet. Magicians do the same by directing your attention to one hand, while retrieving a coin in the other. Beyond pickpockets and magicians, there are many situations in the professional environment in which the question of what people do next is one that you can answer reasonably well – and your prediction of what they do next offers you an advantage.

In Table 7.1 you will find some examples of common workplace situations. The left column provides the context and the right column indicates what people are likely to do next. Before examining the table in detail, try covering the right column and generating your own answer to the question 'What do people do next?' in this situation.

Did you find that you were able to identify some of the common behavioural patterns in those situations? The purpose of this exercise is to start you thinking about the standard, recurring behavioural patterns you can observe – particularly those that are common to large groups of people in professional situations you encounter often. The more you think about and try to identify these patterns, the more you will see them. As you increase your awareness of behavioural inertia, you will increase your ability to predict what comes next – and to use the inertia to your advantage.

TABLE 7.1: Analysis of Inertia in common workplace situations

Context	Inertia *(i.e., how people behave in this situation)*
Introductions: You are in a meeting. Attendees at the meeting are asked to introduce themselves. How will the meeting attendees respond?	Most people at the meeting will be wondering what to say at the same time as speaking. This will be evident in statements such as 'hmmm… what else…?' or through hesitancy as they talk. At least some of those people will tell you where they are from, what they do for a job and whether or not they have any pets, kids or hobbies. This can take quite a long time. If one of the first people to speak adopts a specific format (job title, pets, hobbies, kids), this increases the likelihood that others will follow the same format. It's easier just to do what someone ahead of you did.
Questions at a conference: You are at an event or conference. A keynote speaker has just finished addressing a large audience. The host takes over the microphone to thank the speaker and ask the audience whether or not anyone has any questions. What does the audience do next?	Whether the conference is live or virtual, no one in the audience will react for at least 20 seconds. Eventually one person will raise their hand. While that person is speaking, other people will start to put up their hands. Some of the people who take the microphone will talk rather than ask questions and some will ask two or more questions at the same time.
Job interview: You are being interviewed by a panel for a job. You are the last candidate to be interviewed, not to mention the least experienced. How will the panel perceive your interview?	By the time of your interview, your interviewers will be tired. Further, because they have seen every candidate except one, they have probably already made up their minds. Several panel members will therefore perceive your interview as a courtesy. One of the panel members may even excuse themselves just as you are admitted – because he/she perceives their job has finished and they can go and take a call or do something else now.

APPLYING THE PRINCIPLE OF INERTIA TO
INFLUENCING PEOPLE AND OUTCOMES

The application of this principle to a given situation involves two steps:

Step 1: Identify what inertia exists in the situation you want to influence.

- What is the context, who is involved and how are they most likely to behave?
- What can you predict about the behaviour of people on average in the situation you have chosen? List out a few possible scenarios.
- If you happen to know any of the people involved, ask yourself what you have previously observed about their reactions in similar situations. What is a typical reaction for them?
- Now – to bring this to life – if you were on a game show to win a prize with your predictions, which of these scenarios is most likely?

Step 2: Now ask: If this is an accurate prediction, what is your best possible move?

- Having mapped out what has a reasonable likelihood of occurring, how can you use that knowledge to take advantage of the situation?
- If you are accurate in your predictions of how people will behave, what would be the best way to respond when you see those behaviours occurring?

THE ADVANTAGES OF SEEING WHAT OTHERS DON'T SEE

One key advantage of assessing the behavioural inertia of the situation you want to influence is that the behaviour involved is largely automatic or unconscious. The players in the scenario are likely to execute their behaviours without much upfront planning or conscious choice about what they are doing or about to do. In contrast, you have the potentially massive advantage of being able to plan in advance how you wish to respond under the circumstances that most people will simply react to.

A second advantage that you derive from applying the inertia principle to analyze a situation and plan your actions in advance is that you will avoid the paralysis often experienced when someone knows they are going into an unfair situation.

Let us take the case of the job interview that is the third example mentioned in Table 7.1. In this scenario, you know you will be going into an interview in which you have two disadvantages: you are less experienced than other candidates, and you will be the last person interviewed. Most people would be tempted to think of the situation as 'unfair' and would spend energy wondering if they can change the order in which they are to be interviewed. This is wasted energy because you cannot change these aspects of your situation. However, when armed with the Principle of Inertia, you would say instead 'given that the interviewers will be tired, and given that the candidates before me will have been more experienced, what do I need to say and do to enable the panel to perceive me as a better choice?' Hence the conditions of the situation that people label as 'unfair' and that lead to de-motivation and inaction becoming the boundary conditions within which you will plan to succeed. The same applies when dealing with a more senior manager whom you perceive to be unfair. He or she may well be unfair, but are they predictable? If so, then at least you can use this predictability to your advantage.

Let's revisit the examples in Table 7.1 and examine how you might use these insights on inertia to have more influence over the situation than you would have without such insights. In Table 7.2 we will examine the common situation of heading into a meeting that is either a new group of people or has a new person joining the team.

TABLE 7.2: Leveraging Inertia during introductions at a meeting

Situation 1	*You are in a meeting.*
	Attendees at the meeting are asked to introduce themselves.

Opportunities based on Inertia	Whenever you go into a new meeting situation there is a high probability that people will be asked to introduce themselves. This can also happen when a new member joins an established group. Always go to such a meeting with three to four sentences of prepared introduction, practised so that you can deliver it confidently and clearly.
	When others are speaking off the top of their heads and rambling, you will stand out. Further, the series of unconnected details that your peers will likely provide will be less memorable than the clearly spoken statement you will make.
How to prepare	Prepare a three- to four-line statement with the following characteristics:
	• Express your name very clearly. Other people may be speaking English as a second or third language and you want to be sure they remember it.
	• One to two sentences establishing your expertise or authority (see Principle One: *Status*). Do not automatically revert to your job title to do this. A better statement might be 'I am new to Porsche, but I worked for three years at McKinsey', or 'Last week I executed my first major initiative on our top brand'.
	• One to two sentences that render you likeable in some way (see also Principle Three: *Affiliation*) without undermining the credibility of your expertise/authority. For example, 'I am happy to have the opportunity to meet more people in our company – such as you, Claude, I have heard great things about your work'.
	Practise those lines out loud several times in advance of the meeting so they will be easier to say even if you are nervous when everyone looks at you. It is also important to speak clearly and loudly enough so that everyone can hear you easily (see also Principle Nine: *Execution*).

TABLE 7.3: Leveraging Inertia to network during question time

Situation 2	*You are at an event or conference that could be used as a networking opportunity.* *A keynote speaker has just finished addressing a large audience.*
Opportunities based on Inertia	You have an opportunity to make a connection with the keynote speaker as well as the other important audience members, but it will take some bravery. The alternative approach to networking – waiting in the coffee area and attempting to introduce yourself to people – is a totally hit-and-miss approach. It is also what most other people hoping to connect with someone important will be doing. Networking is much more effective when interesting people come to you instead of you being part of the crowd that goes to them. Take advantage of this inertia to make that happen.
How to prepare	Prepare in advance one impactful, clear, and simple question for the keynote speaker or panel member. Ideally, make a very brief reference to his or her research or work to suggest you have some knowledge in this field and to build an affiliation with the speaker (Principle One: *Status* and Principle Three: *Affiliation*).
	If the session is virtual, be ready to raise your hand or unmute yourself immediately there is an opportunity to ask a question. If the session is live, take a seat near the front so you will be seen easily by everyone during question time. As the session comes to an end, rehearse your question and be ready to put your hand up immediately the opportunity arises so the host has no choice but to give you the microphone (yours will be the only hand in the air in those first crucial seconds).
	Given that you will be the first person to speak, every single person in the audience will hear you (this will not be true for subsequent people who ask a question, because the audience will become more bored the longer that questions continue). Now stand up straight, address the speaker directly, speak loudly and very clearly and stick to the script. If you execute this well, you will not only stand out to all audience members, but you may also well have a pretext for approaching the keynote speaker one-on-one.

Look ahead in your calendar right now. Can you see a meeting on your horizon at which you could practise this technique? The more often you practise preparing in this way for a meeting, the easier it will become for you to remember to prepare.

In Table 7.3 we examined how you can use question time during a conference or speaker event to practise effective networking.

Here are three real-life examples of the application of this type of behavioural inertia that I have coached others to execute:

Example 1. Three master's degree students at an education conference had several senior people come to talk to them after a speaker session. Each student had prepared a specific question for a specific panel member at one of the popular sessions, making brief reference to one of his or her publications. Additionally, the conference organizer wrote to the head of their master's programme to comment on how well they had represented their business school. Not only did this boost the professional reputation of those students within a relevant community – the head of their programme had a concrete example to use in subsequent letters of recommendation for them.

Example 2. At a business seminar, a young professional addressed the Head of Learning & Development for a major corporation who had just given a talk. The speaker had (predictably) lamented that companies were not doing enough to develop their employees' skills. The young man invited the speaker to his workplace to witness the unique solution to this problem that he had personally implemented at work. The whole audience was listening and thus the speaker had no choice but to agree. This resulted in a meeting between the two (for which the young professional prepared well). He was eventually offered a job at the larger company.

Example 3. A mid-level manager addressed the President of the World Bank at a conference of 600 people with a question specifically mentioning last week's *Economist* article about the World Bank. It was the very first question at the start of a two-day conference and everyone there heard it. Although the Head of the Bank left after the panel session, for the rest of the day attendees from all over the world approached the manager and introduced themselves, assuming she was far more important than she was. She was invited to attend dinner with several key players in the industry, where they expressed a desire to keep in touch.

In all these cases, the individuals mentioned could have simply attended the meeting, had a nice time, then gone home, all without ever realizing they had missed a significant opportunity to stand out in a crowd and grow their personal networks.

Finally, in Table 7.4 we will examine how to use your knowledge about behavioural inertia in a job interview situation to enable you to prepare in a way that helps you stand out.

In a real-life example of this specific situation, a good friend of mine was indeed the final candidate to be interviewed among a pool of people with much more experience than her. In fact, her only experience in that specific position was that she had been acting in the role for the past eight months. I coached her so that she was prepared to highlight the proof that she could deliver the results needed in that role, given that was exactly what she had been doing for at least eight months. At the end of the interview process, the panel could not overcome the inertia associated with the fact that other candidates had almost 15 years of experience. When the hiring manager called to express his apologies and reassure her that she was a highly valued figure in the company, she graciously accepted the outcome but asked for a small pay rise instead.* She got it.

---

* As per Principle Four: *Value Framing,* in comparison with the large promotion a person was just denied, awarding a small pay rise can seem quite reasonable

TABLE 7.4: Leveraging Inertia during an 'unfair' job interview

Situation 3	*You are being interviewed by a panel for a job.* *You are the last candidate to be interviewed, not to mention the least experienced.*
Opportunities based on Inertia	Candidates who walk into a situation such as this will immediately notice its disadvantages and that can lead to a downward spiral in confidence. If, instead, you have correctly predicted the situation you now face, you may receive a boost in confidence by seeing that you were correct and that at least you are prepared for exactly this situation. You know in advance you are the least experienced candidate, so your preparation must involve framing your strengths so that you avoid 'years of experience' as the benchmark reference (Principle Four: *Value Framing*). Hiring managers generally fall back on the criterion of 'x years of experience' because it is an easy statement to make and because they assume that someone with *that* many years of experience will be able to do the job in question. The hiring manager thus avoids the very great inconvenience of having to work out what business results they want to see from the person in the job. Your objective must be the opposite: bring attention back to the deliverables for the position and give everyone confidence that you can deliver the results they want to see, so that years of experience become less relevant.
How to prepare	You will need to prepare by determining what key results management expects this position to deliver using any sources available to you (e.g., talking to others in the company to get some perspective). Now consider how you could prove to an interviewer that you are capable of delivering each of those results. For example, have you done the same thing but in a different situation (perhaps under tougher circumstances)? You also know that the interviewers are tired. This makes it even more important that you are prepared appropriately, so that you can take the lead if needed, or possible. A passive approach of waiting for them to lead the entire process only puts more effort onto them. Without overstepping the bounds of clearly demonstrated respect, how can you take some of the effort away from them? For example, could you say 'I know it is tiring to conduct so many interviews. With your permission, would you allow me to address an important question that you might have?' Provided they appear open to this approach, a statement like this enables you to take some leadership over the interview and introduce some of the key messages you want to deliver. Finally, tired interviewers will find it even more difficult to concentrate on long statements that change direction and include unnecessary details. This makes it all the more important that you have practised delivering your key messages so they are crisp, clear and strong. Remember to make your statements easy to understand (Principle Five: *Effort*).

Once again, it is important to emphasize that preparing in the manners outlined above cannot *guarantee* a win. Influence is not a magic spell or a brainwashing button. Developing your skills in influencing people and outcomes in a productive, relationship-building manner will nonetheless result in a pattern of greater success when using these principles than you would achieve without using them.

How can you be accurate in predicting Inertia?

The good news about your efforts to predict people's behaviour in common social situations is that science suggests we can do a reasonable job simply by trying to be accurate. For example, scientists at Stanford and Columbia universities showed that people who were shown pictures of others and asked to make judgements about those people were able to make accurate statements – and used more of their brains – than participants shown the exact same pictures and asked simply whether the picture was taken indoors or outdoors.[14] In a significant overview of research on predicting behaviour, Frith & Frith[15] concluded we have evolved special purpose mechanisms for forecasting social interactions such that our brains are well equipped to predict social behaviour. In fact, many studies indicate that we are generally more accurate in predicting other people's behaviour than in predicting our own reaction to a situation. This is because we embellish self-predictions with a positive spin ('of course I would help that person!').[16] We also predict others' future behaviour based on their past behaviour (which is often accurate), but predict our own future behaviour based on our current aspirations (not so accurate).[17, 18]

One key factor is to keep your focus on identifying the **most likely behaviour** of the people in the situation. Here, 'most likely' must be distinguished from what you *want* them to do (your sincere wish), what you think they *should* do (the optimal reaction) and what you believe *you* would do. Instead, ask 'if my goal is to predict what is most likely to happen in this situation, what are the possible answers?'

You can also improve your accuracy by keeping your focus on **observable behaviour**. Think in terms of external, observable behaviours that can be seen (instead of motivations or attitudes that cannot). If you look again at the examples of Inertia in Table 7.1, you will now notice that they all involve behaviour that can be physically observed.

Another important factor is to attempt to recall **actual incidents that you have observed** in the past. In aiming to recall actual incidents and actual observed behaviours you are more likely to be data-based in your assessment, instead of just trying to guess what might happen. It is by focusing on observable behaviour and developing an interest in observing how people react within common workplace situations that you will improve your skill in this area over time.

This is not to say that our best guesses will always be accurate. In particular, stereotypes about people that derive from our classification of them according to a label (low socioeconomic status, race, nationality, gender, age) more often than not lead to biased and inaccurate predictions about how they will respond to a given situation.[19,20,21] After making your assessment of the predicted inertia in a situation, consider whether or not your predictions simply derive from a stereotype rather than from patterns of behaviour you have personally witnessed regularly. In general, you are more likely to be accurate if you think in terms of situations that occur frequently in your working environment (such that you will have more observational data in your memory bank) and reactions that appear to be true for most people most of the time. The more you can base your predictions on real, observed data instead of top-of-mind guessing, the more accurate you will eventually become.

GET STARTED IN THE NEXT WEEK

As with any complex skill, the method for developing expertise is to start with a small first step, establish some capability, then take another step forward. Begin by thinking about the working week ahead. Identify inertia moments when the people around you are likely to be unprepared or indecisive. By identifying this in advance, you can use the pauses in group inertia to take the lead, or to deliver a prepared response, causing you to stand out among your peers. Practise making predictions, observing what happens and taking advantage of any correct predictions during less important meetings so that you will gain capability you can use eventually during more important meetings.

When using the principle of inertia, do not set yourself up so you are **absolutely relying** on your prediction to be 100 per cent accurate. You cannot expect to be fully accurate every time. Even if you knew for a fact that 90 per cent of the cake-eating population on the planet loves chocolate cake, that would not mean that bringing a chocolate cake for your colleague's birthday will guarantee that he or she will eat a piece. This particular colleague might be allergic to chocolate, or gluten, or might be already uncomfortably full. The fact you did not achieve your desired outcome does not mean that your strategy was a bad one, because even a terrific strategy does not pay out every single time. In general, applying the principle of inertia as described here will result in greater influence over situations and people than you would have without it – and that is the definition of a winning strategy.

BETTER THAN YESTERDAY: USING AWARENESS TO OVERCOME BIAS

As highlighted in Frith & Frith's review,[15] one of the ways in which our brains attempt to predict the behaviour of others is by classifying them as members of a group. Once we perceive an individual as belonging to a group about which we have pre-programmed expectations, the same expectations and predictions are transferred to that individual, often with little or no conscious scrutiny as to whether or not these assumptions are valid for that particular person. This process is hardwired in the brain's amygdala.

For example, we register a physiological stress response when viewing the faces of people who have different racial features from our own.[22] Once upon a time, this ability to react with 'fight or flight' at a subconscious level after classifying a stranger as a member of an enemy tribe would have helped us survive. Today, the same reaction can be measured in our brains, even though the people who look very different from ourselves might be our colleagues, customers, or managers, rather than murderous invading barbarians.

For these reasons, assumptions that can be perceived as racist or sexist are not necessarily sourced from inherently prejudiced beliefs (though this is unfortunately sometimes the case). Instead, they can originate from the innately human behaviour of making assumptions that are informed by stereotypes or cultural expectations. Indeed, the only prerequisite for making biased assumptions about other people's behaviour is simply having a functioning human brain. As a result, unless we are actively taking steps to overcome racist, sexist, and other stereotyped assumptions about other people, we must assume we are making them. While there are some who will argue that stereotype-driven assumptions 'work' or have benefits on occasion, it is nonetheless becoming increasingly evident that such implicitly biased assumptions made by leaders and managers who distribute resources such as promotions, pay packages, government funding and healthcare services continue to result in ongoing inequality and double standards, and even put people's lives at risk.[23, 24]

ILLUSTRATION OF PRINCIPLE SEVEN (*INERTIA*) FIGURE 7

FIGURE 7: As individuals, members of a community, and even members of a species, we execute many predictable behavioural patterns – as if our behaviour were driven by inertia that is difficult to stop once it begins.

Key takeaways

- Human behaviour comes with a force of inertia driving behaviour into identifiable patterns or sequences in response to certain social or contextual stimuli.

- As a result, people's likely reaction in common situations can be relatively predictable, and you can use that predictability to help you exert influence on people and outcomes.

- In general, inertia-driven behaviours are executed without much upfront planning or conscious choice. In contrast, you have the potentially massive advantage of being able to plan in advance how you want to respond. This will enable you to be active and decisive when other people will be inactive and indecisive. You can use the pauses in group inertia to take the lead and stand out. You can also avoid the paralysis often experienced when people find themselves in an unfair situation or facing an unreasonable manager.

- To ensure accuracy, make sure to focus on the **most likely and observable behaviour** of the people in any given situation, rather than what you *want* them to do, think they *should* do or what you believe *you* would do.

Principle Eight

End-Goal Focus (What You Really, Really Want)

Executive summary

Whether we are young children or fully-grown adults, it is seriously difficult to postpone immediate pleasure (like watching another episode) for the sake of pursuing a better but more distant reward (like getting a good night's sleep). This is true even when we are *fully aware* that delayed gratification will result in a better outcome. Often, we do not even notice that we are succumbing to short-term distractions at the expense of our longer-term goals. Behavioural science reveals there are a multitude of ways in which we are pre-programmed to have our attention diverted by the allure of short-term distractions. These could occur in the workplace, for example, as the chance to win an argument, or an opportunity to look clever in front of senior management. Although winning an argument or looking good in a meeting might seem like a victory, that short-term win might sabotage your real goal of gaining the whole team's support for your proposal later on. In this chapter we will define winning as **achieving the outcome you planned for**. Ultimately, you will have far more influence over outcomes in your professional life if you can develop the skills of defining a highly specific end-goal, then staying focused on that specific end-goal, even as everyone around you gets caught up in distractions.

Marshmallows, cuttlefish, and Stanford University

In the 1960s and 70s, Stanford University Professor Walter Mischel and colleagues conducted a series of experiments on delayed gratification that later became known as the 'Marshmallow Test'.[1] In the typical enactment of this experiment, children aged four to six years old were offered the choice between having an immediate treat (e.g. one marshmallow) or waiting for the experimenter to return, whereupon he or she would receive a better reward (e.g. two marshmallows).

Experimenters found that on average the children waited only five to six minutes before giving in to temptation and consuming the treat. Fewer than one-third of participants were able to wait the full 15-minute delay until the experimenter returned.[2] Similar results have been obtained in more recent replications of the test: only 28 per cent of four- to six-year-olds managed a 10-minute wait in a German sample[3] and just 25 per cent of children the same age lasted through a 20-minute wait in a Brazilian study[4] (although a sample of Cameroonian children displayed spectacular self-control, see[3]). Variations of this test have since been expanded not only to other cultures, but also to the animal kingdom: Chimpanzees have been able to wait up to 12 minutes for candy to accumulate[5] and cuttlefish can wait for just over two minutes to obtain a better food reward.[6]

Since then, the marshmallow test has grown to assume the stature of a divining rod for predicting a child's future success. Follow-up studies on Mischel's original cohort of children indicated that those who had been able to sustain the waiting period – thereby 'passing' the marshmallow test – went on to have more successful lives than those who did not.[7,8] While it is undoubtedly true that the ability to delay immediate gratification and practice self-control enables people to achieve a wide range of long-term goals,[9,10,11] recent studies cast doubt on the probability that a kindergartener's marshmallow test results carry much significance in predicting success in adulthood, particularly among children of lower socioeconomic status.[12,13] Nonetheless Mischel's studies serve to remind us of two important points: 1) a sample of children taken from the Bing Nursery School at Stanford University is probably not representative of wider society in many ways, and 2) withstanding immediate temptation is extremely difficult for young children.

Of course, it is not only young children who find it hard to delay immediate gratification in pursuit of bigger goals: as adults, we are surrounded by situations in which we frequently succumb to alluring impulses. We choose streaming the next episode over studying for an exam or going for a drink over going to the gym. People in debt make short-term financial choices that are illogical in relation to their longer-term goals[14] and self-control failure occurs more frequently later in the day as tiredness sets in.[15]

The number one question is this: given how hard it is for us to overcome immediate temptation when we are *fully aware* that taking a quiet pass will bring us a better outcome, how much more difficult is it when we *do not even realize* we are being distracted from our actual intended goal?

ALL THE WAYS WE FORGET ABOUT OUR END-GOAL

It's common for workplace meetings to get derailed. What starts as a group of capable and committed professionals getting together either online or face-to-face to make simple decisions somehow changes course and runs in an unexpected direction. Sometime during the various interactions, the group gets distracted from the original objective and devotes its collective allotment of time and energy to an entirely different topic. This might happen because someone hijacks the agenda to discuss a different idea, or because an unplanned debate consumes more time than anticipated, or because there are external events affecting people's moods (e.g., a department downsizing or a record heatwave). Whether attendees feel the derailed meeting was enjoyable or a waste of time, a meeting cannot achieve its objective unless there *was a specific objective, and it was indeed achieved.*

As we saw in the discussion of delayed gratification above, it's just so much easier for humans to focus on short-term immediate matters than to maintain focus on a more distant, bigger picture. In fact, behavioural science reveals that there are a multitude of ways in which we are **pre-programmed** to be distracted from achieving longer-term outcomes.

We are hardwired to be distracted frequently

We have all experienced the frustration of intending to give a task our full attention, only to find that a message alert, hunger pang or some other interruption hijacks our attention and leads us down a less productive path. We tend to think of being focused as the morally superior state and being distracted as indicative of some sort of problem. In fact, recent research measuring heart rate and brain activity has demonstrated that both humans and non-human primates experience neural oscillations that require us to re-focus our attention at a microlevel on a second-by-second basis.[16] **In other words, being open to distraction most of the time is our natural state.**

We can't focus on many things at once

At this stage in the book, you will have read several times that we have limited mental processing capability and therefore limited attention to bestow upon the social and environmental stimuli around us. It bears repeating because, essentially, this is the root mechanism at the heart of all principles of influence. It is only because our brains take shortcuts – equating height with value or calculating the size of an object relative to its surroundings – that we can influence people's perceptions by tapping into those shortcuts.

In the case of visual information, our brains sift through the millions of details we could be looking at to identify what we think we need, what we can save for later and what can be deleted altogether. This phenomenon was demonstrated in a now-famous experiment in which 192 undergraduates were asked to watch short videos of six people passing a basketball to each other.[17] Three of the players were wearing white T-shirts and three were in black T-shirts. Participants were asked to count how many times the people wearing one of these two colours passed the ball. As a result of focusing on ball-passing behaviour, only 54 per cent of participants noticed an unexpected event (e.g., a woman wearing a gorilla suit) appearing for five seconds in the 75-second-long video. Further, this proportion dropped to just 8 per cent when the woman wore the (fully black) gorilla suit and participants were asked to focus on white-T-shirt players only. In a replication with greater real-world consequences, Irish researchers found that fewer than 20 per cent of drivers who were engaged in the mental act of judging whether or not their vehicle could fit between two parked cars were unable to notice an animal or small child walking into the path of the cars they were driving.[18] **When we have been instructed to focus our attention against one set of stimuli, we are less likely to notice new information that falls outside of that attention spotlight.**

We get distracted because of our emotional state

Generally, we tend to consider that our cognitive skills and our emotional reactions are two distinct realms. We debate responding to a problem either with 'our heart' or with 'our head'. Although this may be a useful means of describing personal experience, a large-scale review of research in neuroscience indicates that emotions are not distinct from cognitive skills, but rather act as a dimension of cognitive skills, like shelves that underlie glassware.[19] More simply, our current emotional state affects where we put our attention.

This effect was demonstrated in an experiment conducted with master's degree students taking an Operations Management course in Dubai.[20,21] Researchers found that a group of students given a fun experience at the start of a three-hour class experienced a positive mood – and maintained that positive feeling throughout the whole teaching period, even when the topics and teaching style changed. A second group of students with no such fun start began the teaching period in a neutral mood and maintained that neutral mood over the same period and subjects. Two days later, when both groups were tested spontaneously on the topics they had covered, the first group significantly outperformed the second on all the topics from that class. This study demonstrated that even relatively minor variations in mood (e.g., from positive to neutral) can affect the extent to which we pay attention to what is happening.

Consider this in your next meeting or video call. Chances are that at least some of the people who appear to be focused – and neutral in demeanour – are not taking in as much information as you might hope. In summary, **the narrow focus of our attention is pulled in different directions based on our emotional state**.

We are heavily distracted by the prospect of a reward

Have you ever gone into a supermarket to buy something unexciting like toothpaste and found yourself leaving with a fresh croissant that smells amazing? Perhaps you sat down to write an email and found yourself checking social media? These behaviours occur because – on top of the fact that we are easily distracted – we are even more likely to be distracted by stimuli that appear to offer greater or more immediate reward than whatever we are supposed to be doing. Researchers demonstrate this in the lab by showing that people are better at remembering word sequences they have been told are 'worth more points'[22], and they measure it in real world settings when people are distracted away from their current tasks by enticing stimuli such as food, money or social approval. In a recent meta-analysis of 91 different studies from around the world, researchers confirmed that our brains focus on rewards that occur around us even if that focus is counterproductive to our current goals or current performance.[23] Indeed, a study of pedestrians crossing busy roads in Melbourne, Australia, found that 20 per cent of people continued to look at their smartphone screens despite the serious risk of critical accidents occurring.[24] **We are so predictably distracted away from our current task by apparently rewarding stimuli that behavioural scientists have coined the term 'reward-driven distraction'.**

We get distracted by being competitive

You may recall that Social Comparison Theory[25] was introduced back in Chapter Two (*Social Imitation*) when we examined the vast extent to which our behaviour is subconsciously affected by that of the people around us. It is precisely because we are continually driven to compare ourselves to others that we are so easily drawn into competitions and arguments, even when that engagement is a total distraction. Napoleon used our competitive drive to influence men into risking their lives for the privilege of being distinguished among their peers, famously stating 'a soldier will fight long and hard for a bit of coloured ribbon'. A study of CEOs in New Zealand found their behaviour changed during periods when it was possible to receive a knighthood or damehood, even though those awards carry no certain material benefit – and what they did at those times was detrimental to the firm's performance (and arguably their own bonuses).[26]

In the business world, we consider being competitive as so fundamentally desirable that we literally use the term 'competitive' as if it were unquestionably always a positive attribute of a person or their behaviour. In contrast, consider how easy it would be to divert meeting attendees into irrelevant competitions (e.g., over who works the most on vacation), if my actual intention were to reduce the time available to discuss an issue I wanted to avoid. We get drawn into arguments and competitions because beating another person feels rewarding – but winning is not just an occasional distraction, it might even thwart your long-term goals by leaving people you need feeling hostile or defensive.

Finally, when we allow 'winning' or 'beating those around us' to function as our default end-goal, we allow what we want to achieve to be defined by what others are doing. In effect, **we are failing to set our own goals**. In contrast, a sports psychology study of college swimmers found that athletes who set personal performance goals that were 1) important to the individual and 2) highly specific, achieved better performance improvements than those encouraged with the default approach of being 'more competitive'.[27] **It might feel rewarding to act competitively, however this competition**

can easily operate as an irrelevant distraction from what you want to achieve.

DEFINING YOUR SPECIFIC END-GOAL

The distinction between activities and results

What matters most in a business: the activities people do or the results they achieve? If you have ever been an entrepreneur and had to pay your employees' salaries out of the limited income your new company generates, you will be able to answer this question in a microsecond. If you are paying a room full of people to keep themselves busy with activities, then you have an expensive day-care facility for adults. However, if you are paying people to deliver results, you may have one of the key building blocks of a successful business. The problem is that it is so much easier for us to focus on the short-term and tangible, and thus a list of activities we want to get done, instead of addressing the more difficult question of exactly what outcome we are aiming to achieve in the longer term.

Without disciplined thinking, the distinction can be difficult, especially when performing an activity and achieving a result might look similar. Consider that a tennis player hitting balls across a net might be aiming to improve his or her forehand shot or might be trying to win a game. The activities can look much the same, but unless the player is sure exactly which of these two outcomes they are trying to achieve, they cannot follow the most effective route to the goal.

A very specific outcome is a clear target

To use another sports analogy, now imagine an archer firing arrows to hit a target. One approach is to fire off a quiver of arrows in the approximate direction of a number of targets. Another approach is to choose one clearly visible target, then line up every single arrow shot as precisely as possible against that single target. The second approach both improves your chances of hitting a target and ensures that your effort, attention and energy are all focused in the same place.

However, the first approach is how most of us attempt to achieve the things we want: We take a variety of steps that are more or less in the direction of a vague series of distant targets that we haven't taken the time to define precisely. To illustrate, consider how most people approach making a presentation on a given topic. The typical workplace approach is to design a presentation according to factors such as what information needs to be in the presentation and for how long one needs to speak. These are activities, not results. When someone has just given a presentation that was designed in this manner and you ask them what they had planned to achieve from it, they will likely list a number of vague targets such as 'providing all the data for the region', 'impressing my boss' or 'presenting my progress'. The true answer is that they didn't specifically plan to achieve anything – they executed a series of activities that they thought were expected of them under the circumstances (*see also* Principle Two: *Social Imitation*).

Suppose instead that you took the time to define a precise outcome from your next presentation, such as delivering a crucial message that attendees can repeat the next day, influencing a decision in one direction, or creating a specific brand image for yourself in the minds of your manager and colleagues. Like an archer aiming for a single clear target, you would know exactly what outcome you seek. As a result, you could focus your effort, attention and energy against achieving that specific outcome.

Winning is achieving the outcome you planned for

In the same way that it is common for us to execute activities in pursuit of a series of vague goals, it is easy to be distracted into achieving outcomes that are irrelevant. For example, it is easy and even reflexive to see yourself as successful if you beat other people, complete a difficult task or solve a problem. But are these meaningful results, or just activities you got distracted into doing? You can only be sure if you have defined the outcome you want to achieve and that step you are taking now is an essential milestone in achieving it.

APPLYING THE PRINCIPLE OF END-GOAL FOCUS TO INFLUENCING PEOPLE AND OUTCOMES

There are three key steps through which you can apply Principle Eight to increase your ability to influence people and outcomes:

1. **Ensure that you define a clear and specific end-goal.** In line with the study on collegiate swimmers, the end-goal should be important to you, as well as highly specific and appropriate to the situation.

2. **Plan actions that directly target your specific end-goal.** Ask 'if this is what I want to achieve, what do I need to do to maximize the likelihood of that particular outcome?' Think of action steps as being like arrows aimed *precisely* at the target – not vaguely somewhere in the right direction. As illustrated by the undergraduates who could not see a woman in a gorilla suit, once we have defined where we need to focus, we reduce the likelihood we pay attention to new stimuli that fall outside that definition.

3. **Keep your eyes on the prize**. Maintain your focus against your true defined objective irrespective of the many distractions that occur around you. You will need to avoid getting sucked down a different pathway despite your brain's in-built tendency to be distracted by other immediate concerns.

Tables 8.1 and 8.2 provide illustrations of these three steps, drawing on the points established in the chapter's behavioural science overview. These scenarios represent common situations in which the end-goal can be obscured by activities (Table 8.1) or there is a possibility of obtaining so many potential benefits that you fail to define and target one (Table 8.2). In both cases, unless you take the conscious step of defining one clear and specific end-goal against which to focus, the most likely eventuality is that all your well-intentioned activity will fall short of any tangible outcome, just as a quiver of arrows fired roughly in the direction of several distant targets is unlikely to make a hit.

TABLE 8.1: Example 1: Three steps to applying End-Goal Focus when presenting to a client

Note the distinction between 1) being distracted and 2) end-goal focus during each of the three steps listed above

Scenario	*You are a regional account manager for an important client.* Your manager has organized a meeting at which you and the other two regional account managers will present your quarterly results to the client.	
	Distractions	*End-Goal Focus*
Step 1: **Define the** **End-Goal**	It is easy to get distracted by the activities involved in creating slides for your presentation. You must pull together the quarterly data, make clear charts, perhaps even align some aspects of your layout with those of the other account managers. There is a lot to be done!	Whether or not your client is consciously aware of it, the most valuable insight that he or she can take from your presentation is 1) a simple message about a success story in your region, or 2) a data-based insight that suggests how he or she can increase business in the future. This will provide great value to your client and you will stand out as a result.
Step 2: **Target the** **End-Goal**	The list of activities to complete might get even longer if your manager has certain specifications for the presentation. Further, if the meeting is face to face, there might be arrangements such as room booking or catering to organize. All these activities might be necessary, but they are not your end-goal. You are unlikely to get a promotion because you organized a nice meeting with good food.	It is crucial both that you have devised an appropriate insight and that it will be presented in a clear and unmissable manner to your client. No matter how much time all the necessary activities take up, don't postpone identifying the message you want to deliver and planning to ensure you can deliver it during the meeting.
Step 3: **Eyes on** **the Prize**	Everyone around you will be focused on activities and 'making a good impression on the client'. Even your client is likely to be focused on activities – such as viewing the data, getting the most out of the meeting, etc. There is nothing wrong with making a good impression, but it makes a better impression if you have a nice meeting **and** deliver valuable business-building insights at the same time.	Keep the end-goal in mind, both in planning and delivering your presentation. Ensure the key message will be delivered clearly to your client even if you end up with less time than scheduled because other presentations overrun or the client interrupts with unrelated questions.

TABLE 8.2: Example 2: Three steps to applying End-Goal Focus in a complex situation

Note the distinction between 1) being distracted and 2) end-goal focus during each of the three steps listed above

Scenario	**You are a business consultant**. You have been hired on a temporary assignment by a local consumer goods distributor. Your job is to help your local client win a regional distribution contract with a famous multinational brand manufacturer. You will join a team of around six people, made up of your client's general manager and several of his or her direct reports, to host a half-day meeting with the regional CEO of the manufacturing company. The CEO will also be joined by several his or her direct reports, so there will be two equally sized teams at the meeting.
	This situation offers many opportunities: 1) You could help your client win the contract, which might result in a bonus payment for this project; 2) You could impress your client in order to win more business from them on future projects; 3) You could impress the team from the big brand name manufacturer and potentially win business from the more well-known company also; 4) You could network with the team from the manufacturer who might be good future contacts.

	Distractions	*End-Goal Focus*
Step 1: Define the End-Goal	There seem to be so many potential benefits, you decide to impress everybody and help win the contract at the same time! Unfortunately, that does not provide a clear outcome against which you can target direct actions.	Your client has already hired you for this project. The most likely benefit you can obtain here is #2 (above) because it is the only one that relies on another party repeating past behaviour choices (see Principle Seven: *Inertia*). Put your focus here.

| **Step 2: Target the End-Goal** | Your vague series of goals (helping to win the contract, impressing your client, impressing the manufacturer) does not allow you to define targeted actions. There is a high likelihood you will engage in well-intentioned activities that achieve little and could even backfire – such as talking too much or attempting to win side arguments in a manner intended to be 'impressive'. | The most important person in the meeting is the member of your client's team with the budget or authority to give you another project. List out what specific actions you could take at this meeting to maximize the likelihood that he or she will perceive you as a valuable asset to the team. |
| **Step 3: Eyes on the Prize** | The fact that the manufacturer is a world-recognized brand name is likely to be distracting. Your brain is likely to subconsciously classify those team members as more important than your team members from the current client. As a result, you run the risk of giving them more attention and treating them with more respect than the team from your actual client. | Keep your focus against the key person on your own team and don't be distracted by the greater apparent status of the larger company's CEO. Your preparation for the meeting and your behaviour in the meeting should be actively aimed at showing your support for your target person, even if other members of your own team get distracted. |

STRATEGIES FOR KEEPING YOUR EYES ON THE PRIZE

By now, it should be clear that you will be more successful and have more influence over your workplace outcomes if you invest the time needed to define a highly specific end-goal and plan targeted action steps aimed directly at this outcome. This is already a major achievement compared with simply allowing ourselves to perform activities under the implicit assumption that we are vaguely headed in the direction of generally positive outcomes.

However, given that it is our natural state to be highly susceptible to distraction, it's probably a good strategy to also arm yourself with some extra tools for maintaining focus. Further, there may be times when you need attention from other people who get distracted and being able to re-focus them on what you need them to do can come in handy. To help you with this, here are a series of science-backed strategies for keeping your eyes on the prize.

Microbreaks

When you need to maintain concentration and focus, one proven technique is to take planned microbreaks away from what you are doing so that you pre-empt your drive to be distracted and can return to being focused more effectively. Microbreaks need to be short and regular in order to have a positive effect. A study of South Korean workers identified that microbreaks that involve a moment of relaxation, or a short social encounter were effective, microbreaks to eat or drink were less so and interruptions that required a shift in cognitive activity to address a different topic had a negative effect.[28] Similarly, if you need to maintain the focus of a team of people in a meeting, it's probably helping your end-goal if you find members of the team occasionally break away from the subject to banter or recount a funny story – so long as it is truly a microbreak and not a change of direction.

Positive emotions

In the behavioural science section of this chapter, we learned that people pay more attention to a subject or activity when they feel positive, compared to if they feel negative or even neutral. As seen in the study of Operations Management students in Dubai, emotional state need not be determined by the current topic, meaning that an experience that generates a positive mood can create a benefit that lasts into the next topic. How can you create a positive mood right at the time you need yourself or others to maintain focus? Would going for a run or walk just before you need to focus be positive for you? Could you start a meeting or introduce your presentation with an experience designed to put attendees in a good mood? The stimulus or experience you use to do this should be subtle and should not in itself function as a distraction. To illustrate the difference: a short uplifting tune, some positive feedback to the audience or an aesthetically designed room can all act as subtle influencers of positive mood in a meeting group. In contrast, a five-minute video of a dog water-skiing will function as a distraction and might eventually be the only thing that anyone remembers about your presentation or meeting.

Reward associations

As we have learned, we are better able to focus on stimuli that appear to be rewarding. How can you state your end-goal in a manner that explicitly amplifies the positive reward it involves? Can you identify inspirational or inherently valuable aspects of the outcome against which you want to focus? See if you can re-phrase your end-goal to make it appear more rewarding than any distractions that occur. Similarly, if you need to focus other people's attention, how can you ensure they perceive the topic as intrinsically wrapped in a reward that matters to them? Once again, the bigger and more explicit the reward aspect appears, the greater the likelihood it will surpass other distractors that might occur.

Write a personal slogan that expresses the end-goal

Consumer products use slogans in advertising because they help people recall important brand attributes when faced with the distracting environment of a supermarket.[29] In the same way, you can design a slogan or a short mantra that captures your specific end-goal in an explicit and positive manner. For example, to take the scenario in Table 8.1, your slogan might be: *'My client needs to know that the initiative was successful, and that more programmes in the same region will generate success'*. Repeating your mantra silently in your head can help protect you from getting drawn into reactions or side arguments that seem appropriate in the moment but detract you from achieving your end goal.

Plan to prevent distracting stimuli

While we may blame technology for distracting us, recall it is our brains that actually distract us – technology just offers a range of stimuli more rewarding than what we are doing right now. As a result, maintaining focus means acting to reduce the occurrence of more interesting stimuli that our minds could latch onto. The most obvious example might seem to be setting your phone to 'do not disturb', although studies have shown that even the mere presence of an unused mobile phone is enough to create divided attention, perhaps because its presence is a reminder of the social invitations you could be missing.[30] If you have any control over the environment in which you (and other people) need to stay focused, consider how to insulate it against the sight or smell of tempting food, entertaining scenes, notifications from Tinder or the sounds of other people having more fun than you.

Start building your skills now

Learning new insights feels like progress, but exactly what are you aiming to achieve? Is your goal simply to 'increase your knowledge', 'improve your skills' or 'finish another chapter of this book', all of which are pretty vague and sound a bit like activities. Instead, why not aim to begin measurable skill development by creating one instance in which you practise applying Principle Eight to a workplace situation in the coming week? Your goal is to have one example in which you actively apply the principle, and the reward is that you will make at least some degree of progress in improving your influencing skills (because you need to actively practise new skills; it is not enough to read about them).

So, right now, start by identifying an upcoming professional situation that requires an investment of your time and effort – whether it's a meeting, an event, a project or just a regular day of work. Next, define an end-goal that is appropriate to that context. Continue into planning the steps that directly target your end-goal, as well as how you intend to keep your eyes on the prize. At this stage, don't get tempted into being overly ambitious with the end-goal. Your true goal for now is to complete a practice session to begin skill development – not to change the whole world (yet!).

BETTER THAN YESTERDAY: APPLYING THE PRINCIPLE OF END-GOAL FOCUS TO FEEL HAPPIER

Our tendency to be easily distracted may have helped us survive the dangers of the prehistoric world – but it does not help us to feel any happier. You might be tempted into believing that daydreaming about your next holiday or thinking about the shoes you want to buy is a simple enough pastime, but research indicates we feel significantly happier when our minds are fully in the present, instead of wandering into the future or reliving the past.

A study by Harvard psychologist and happiness expert Daniel Gilbert of over 2,000 people aged 18 to 88 used a phone app to track what they were doing, what they were thinking about and how happy they felt throughout the day. Results uncovered that a wandering mind was associated with lower happiness, whereas being fully present mentally was more than twice as important in increasing happiness compared with the specific task the person was doing at the time.[31]

Further, the deleterious effect of divided attention on current performance is a species-wide tendency that does indeed include 'digital natives' born in the internet era. In fact, there is evidence from brain studies using functional magnetic resonance imaging (fMRI) that constantly switching between tasks may lead to a person losing the ability to focus on one single task – and may even negatively affect future brain development.[32]

In summary, your ability to drown out constant interruptions to focus your attention on where you are, what you are doing and who you are with right now is probably much more important than you ever previously considered. The skills you develop when practising to apply Principle Eight will not only increase your ability to influence outcomes, but they will also make you a better performer and perhaps even a happier person.

ILLUSTRATION OF PRINCIPLE EIGHT
(*END-GOAL FOCUS*) FIGURE 8

FIGURE 8: Firing multiple arrows at a series of targets is less effective than aiming all your arrows and all your effort at one clear and precise target. Unfortunately, we are easily distracted by multiple targets.

Key takeaways

- There are a multitude of ways in which we are pre-programmed to be distracted away from achieving longer-term outcomes by the allure of short-term rewards. In fact, being open to distraction most of the time is our natural state.

- The focus of our attention is affected by many factors, including our emotional condition, the prospect of reward, or any kind of challenge or competition. However, winning is not beating others: Winning is achieving the outcome you planned for.

- In business, the results people achieve are more important than the activities they do – but activities are easier to focus on because they are concrete and immediate. Instead of performing activities in the belief they will achieve results, start with defining what you want to achieve and then plan the specific steps you must take to get to the outcome you chose.

- There are three key steps to applying Principle Eight: 1) define a clear and specific end-goal, 2) plan actions that directly target that specific end-goal and 3) keep your eyes on the prize to achieve that end-goal even while everyone else gets distracted.

- Accept that humans are highly susceptible to distraction and arm yourself with extra tools for maintaining your focus, including taking microbreaks, remembering a mantra that expresses the end-goal in a rewarding manner and actively reducing opportunities for distractions.

Principle Nine

Execution (The Final 100m)

Executive summary

Making a plan and executing that plan are not the same thing. You could train for years to perform in an Olympic event, but the value of that effort can only be realized when you cross the finish line. Throughout the preceding chapters you have been encouraged to build your influencing skills using an understanding of the social, contextual, and interactive factors that affect outcomes and decision making in workplace situations. The final step in skill development is to consider how specific characteristics of your physical behaviour can add to (or detract from) your influencing power. When you have drawn up an influencing plan using Principles One to Eight, practise executing that plan using the aspects of execution and delivery that are most strongly linked to persuasion: posture, words, message, and voice. The models for each of these elements that have been identified by science as most effective in influencing are significantly different from the default posture, words, content, and voice people use on a daily basis. Practising micro adjustments in your execution must be done in advance because it is too hard to focus both on *what you are saying* and *how you are saying it* in the moment when everyone is looking at you.

A LONG WAY BUT NOT FAR ENOUGH

Back in Principle Four (*Value Framing*), I used the context of average running paces on a treadmill to communicate the enormous achievement involved in running a full marathon in two hours and 20 minutes – the equivalent of maintaining a pace just below a flat-out sprint for 2,110 lengths of a cricket pitch. At the 2004 Olympic Games in Athens, Brazilian athlete Vanderlei de Lima had been running at an even faster pace for almost one hour and 50 minutes. For 15 years, he had been training to represent his country. He was around 85 per cent of the way through the gruelling event, on track for the gold medal, and then he was pushed to the ground by a protester in fancy dress. Despite all the preparation and all the years of suffering, de Lima's example illustrates that you can't win a marathon by running 42km: You have to run 42km and then a further 195 metres. If you don't complete the final stretch, literally years of preparation can be wasted.*

THE LAST 100M IN A WORK ENVIRONMENT

Ever witnessed a star conference presenter, a speaker or a colleague get tripped up at the start of a talk because they couldn't work the technical equipment? Perhaps you provided some insight or analysis to your manager, only to discover that the relevant decision had already been taken? Or maybe you experienced working out the answer faster than everyone else, but received no credit because you did not speak up in time? In a work environment it is easy to forget completely about the final 100m that can have a massive impact on the effectiveness of all the work you have done. As discussed in Principle Eight (*End-Goal Focus*), it is easier to focus on the activities we need to complete than the result we intend to achieve. This is because activities are immediate and tangible, whereas defining a

---

* Fortunately for de Lima, he managed to recover sufficiently to continue the race and still earn a bronze medal. Later, he was also decorated with an athletics award for representing perseverance in the face of adversity

specific end-goal requires more effortful thinking. As a result, when people prepare for a presentation, they tend to invest all their effort into writing the talk or designing the slides (an activity) and pretty much none into practising how the actual out-loud delivery will affect the audience (result).

In the context of influencing people and outcomes, the concept of the last 100m provides a model for tuning up your performance before the execution of your influencing plan. Just as in the presentation example above, it is one thing to use your knowledge of affiliation, value framing or reasoning to plan an influencing attempt and a separate enterprise to deliver it in an effective manner. Whether you plan to execute your influence attempt via email, during an in-person meeting or an online call, Principle Nine provides you with a checklist for examining, practising, and improving the behavioural aspects of execution that can significantly affect your likelihood of success.

FEELING CONFIDENT AND LOOKING CONFIDENT ARE NOT THE SAME THING

Most of us believe we are pretty good at reading body language or facial expressions and thus classifying other people as truthful, deceitful, or confident. In fact, research shows that our belief in our own accuracy when evaluating others is much more robust than our actual accuracy. For example, a wide array of people (including police officers) all perform only slightly better than chance when it comes to detecting a person who is lying, even though they feel confident about their judgements.[1,2] Similarly, as discussed already in Principle One (*Status*), we routinely mistake outward displays of confidence for actual competence. As a result, individuals who are low in competence but high in confidence can lead groups of people to make decisions that are less accurate than those made by the same individuals when they are surveyed on their own.[3] This confusion of confidence with competence occurs because we carry an inherent belief that confident people will stand up straight and 'hold themselves tall'. The amusing reality is that science suggests the opposite is true: People who stand up straight feel more confident and act more confidently. Here, we'll take a whirlwind tour through the science of postural effects and what that means for you when executing your influencing plan.

Power posing and a mega-successful TED Talk

In a now-famous and somewhat controversial experiment, researchers from Harvard and Columbia universities published results showing that adopting a static power pose (upright back, expanded body size, arms held out or upwards) for just two minutes at a time had profound and lasting physiological and psychological effects when compared to people who adopted a contractive pose (leaning inwards, body slouched, arms or legs crossed).[4] The suggestion that power posing resulted not only in feelings of increased self-confidence and power, but also increases in testosterone, decreases in the stress hormone cortisol and an increased willingness to tolerate risk became widely known in the world of social psychology and led study author Dr Amy Cuddy to deliver one of the most-viewed TED Talks of all time.[5] Follow-up studies suggested that a few minutes of power posing before an interview resulted in a greater likelihood of being hired following an interview[6] as well as an increased tolerance to pain,[7] but shortly thereafter criticisms of the power posing literature arose when researchers working with larger sample sizes found no effect of power posing on some of these outcomes (specifically hormone levels and risk-taking behaviour).[8] Much of the criticism appears to be motivated by a jealous reaction to Cuddy's sudden fame, as well as her (probably overstated) suggestion that a few minutes of daily power posing could be a panacea solution for people with 'no status and no power'.[5] Yet, there is still significant value in examining this body of research.

Instead, let's call it an upright, expansive posture

In fact, the effect of body posture on confidence had started to emerge in scientific literature before the term 'power posing' was used by Cuddy and her team. In the first published study in this genre, researchers asked university students to make a list of their personal qualities while sitting in one of two different positions: 1) '*Confident*' (an erect back with your chest pushed out) or 2) '*Doubtful*' (a curved back with your chest slouched forward, probably just like you're doing right now).[9] After completing that list, they were asked to relax their postures and complete a questionnaire containing a wide variety of self-evaluation questions. These included evaluating themselves as good candidates for the job market, good candidates for a job interview and good on-the-job performers. The results found that those who had adopted the upright posture were significantly more confident in their own value as candidates or employees compared to those who had written about themselves in the slouched position.

In a recent replication of this experiment with German school children in the fourth grade, researchers found that children who were required to spend just one full minute in an expansive, high-power pose reported higher self-esteem and more positive feelings towards themselves and others than those who were asked to adopt a contractive, slumped low-power pose for one minute.[10] Another recent meta-analysis conducted by researchers at the Aarhus University in Denmark and covering 73 studies from around the world found robust evidence for positive changes in mood and behaviour when people actively adopted an expansive, upright posture compared to a contractive, slouched position.[11] In short, there is plenty of evidence that how you hold your body can significantly affect your mood, confidence and behaviour.

FACTOR 1: AN UPRIGHT, EXPANSIVE POSTURE

In general, the posture that appears to offer the most benefits relative to the widest array of professional contexts involves:

1. Straight back (with spine stretched);
2. Shoulders back;
3. An overall erect and upright upper body;

4. Face and eyes level and oriented straight forward;
5. Arms or legs extended rather than crossed or contracted.

These postural elements might seem like small adjustments, but realistically this overall position is significantly different from the typical posture that we adopt when we are unconscious of how we are sitting or standing. In fact, the studies confirming the positive benefits of this posture started with a baseline measure of how participants sat, stood and walked and demonstrated that the 'upright, expansive' posture they were asked to adopt for the experiment was indeed significantly different from participants' baseline postures before the experiment began.

Canadian researchers working with men and women in their 20s and 30s found they could generate more positive thoughts that lasted for longer when sitting in an upright posture, compared to a slumped pose. Incredibly, each of the two groups adopted their respective positions for only one minute at a time, with one minute of rest, repeated for four sets.[12] Experiments by researchers in New Zealand similarly compared people in a prescribed upright and slightly expanded position to a hunched, downwards-looking position when sitting for 30 minutes[13] and walking for 13 minutes.[14] During each of these experiments, participants were asked to perform two impromptu tasks previously proven to induce stress (such as answering an interview question to attain their dream job). Researchers measured their mood, physiological reactions and actual task performance. The results demonstrated that when faced with stress, the upright expanded posture enabled participants to maintain a positive and energetic mood, reduced negative, dull or sleepy feelings, improved feelings of self-esteem and reduced negative stress responses. Moreover, upright participants performed better in that they were able to speak more easily and used more positive words during task performance. In summary, it appears that the postural elements outlined in the model above enable people to feel better and perform better when faced with the kind of stressful tasks that routinely occur in the workplace.

The benefits of an upright, expanded posture spread beyond how you feel and how you perform into how you are perceived by others. In a German study involving more than 2,000 respondents asked to evaluate people from their photographs, both men and women who were sitting or standing in an upright, expanded posture (back straight, shoulders back, elbows out) were rated as significantly more competent than those in a slouched, contracted position.[15] Similarly, an American field study in which 3,000 people reacted to photographs on a dating app found that photographs in which people's arms, legs or body length were extended or stretched out were more likely to be chosen as more attractive than the same people photographed in hunch, contracted or closed positions.[16]

Finally, although studies continue to show that adopting a classic high-power pose (e.g., sitting with feet on the table, or standing and leaning across a table on extended arms) results in increased feelings of power and self-esteem,[17] even when performed alone at home,[18] this posture would likely be interpreted as an overt attempt to express dominance when performed in the presence of other people. As such, you run the risk of inducing a negative emotional response in the people you are attempting to influence. An upright, expansive posture is the goal here – don't go putting your feet on anybody's desk!

Factor 2: The (simple and familiar) words you choose

When examining Principle Four (*Value Framing*), we saw that you can influence how people perceive an object by controlling the context within which it occurs or the examples to which it is compared. In the same way, behavioural science shows you can influence how people perceive your message by careful choice of the words you use to express an idea. There are two key factors in word choice to consider:

1. **Use simple words in place of more complex or difficult words**: In a study of the impression created by specific word choice, researchers wrote two versions of the exact

same argument. One version used simple terms (e.g., 'when workers unions are strongly united'), while the other expressed the same content in difficult, technical terms (e.g., 'when institutional support for anti-regime actors is strong'). People who read the simple argument rated the author as significantly more competent and more trustworthy than those who read the complex version. Moreover, when asked about the personality of the writer, those who read the simple version commented that the author was open-minded and warm, whereas the complex version led readers to view the author as cold and calculating.[19]

2. **Choose words that resonate with the influence target**: A review of 25 years of management research into words that drive action in organizations and companies found the key feature of messages that influence people to act was the use of words, ideas and terminology that match the interests and agenda of the audience.[20] Sociology researchers call this the 'resonance' of the words you choose to express your idea.[21]

Resonance comes in two forms: cognitive or emotional.[22] Cognitive resonance occurs when the words or structure used match the audience's needs, expectations, or beliefs. It is influential because it attracts attention through unconscious recognition that your message meets the receiver's needs. For example, researchers closely examined over 36,000 reports written by analysts in the biotechnology and pharmaceutical industries. They found that analysts who consistently structured their reports in line with the key needs of investors (e.g. a stated goal of identifying good investment opportunities) were overwhelmingly rated by those investors as being the best analysts, irrespective of how good their investment advice had been.[23] Moreover, the same analysts were most likely to be voted as one of the best analysts of the year by readers of *Institutional Investor* magazine – an outcome the researchers noted could bring a salary increase of up to $1 million per year!

Emotional resonance occurs when the words or structure you use align with the audience's aspirations, desires, or passions. This kind of resonance is felt by the audience. It overlaps with Principle Four (*Value Framing*), in that you might express one thing (such as a delay) in terms of a currency that matters more to the audience (such as minutes of their evening that were wasted). It can also include content designed to evoke an emotional reaction and a sense of identification in the listener – which leads to a more positive perception of the message. For example, research has shown that positive evaluations of a brand are correlated strongly with the emotional (but not the factual) content of advertising.[24] Emotional resonance has also been used to explain the success of Donald Trump's 2016 presidential campaign because voters did not care about the feasibility of his proposals, just the emotion of how they made them feel.[22]

FACTOR 3: HAVE AN OVERALL MESSAGE (THAT BRINGS SOMETHING NEW)

Have a message that summarizes your communication
You are more likely to galvanize people into action if what you say continues to affect them after they hear you say it. That is more likely to happen if you give them a short summary message to remember. Just as advertisers use jingles and taglines to leave consumers with a message that drives both recognition and recall,[25] aim to summarize your communication in one to three sentences. Of course, your influencing plan likely involves more communication than just a few sentences, but the key to delivering a consistent message to all listeners is to provide that summary message pre-packaged for them to take away. If you can't state the overall message of your own communication, then there is a good chance you are not communicating a consistent overall message, but instead leaving the audience to identify a message for themselves. This is something they probably will not do, given that human brains don't like being asked to work unless they really need to (see Principle Five: *Effort*).

New, but not too different

Researchers from Cornell University analyzed posts on an online debating forum called ChangeMyView on Reddit.[26] The forum invites users to post their beliefs and explain why they hold these opinions – and other users to respond in an attempt to change their minds. Analysis identified that the most successful opinion-changing arguments were communicated in words similar to those used by the original opinion holder (creating resonance) and in addition provided new information. Influencing power increased when a user included something that was not known before in the argument.

Factor 4: Practise how you use your voice – out loud

In both face-to-face and online meetings or presentations, the audience's reaction to what you say out loud is significantly affected by how you sound when you speak. In this section you will learn to identify the key features of a person's voice that can make them significantly more influential – and even more likely to win an election!

However you speak – normally, and when thinking hard – it is not optimal for influencing others

Whatever volume, pitch, pace or intonation happens when you open your mouth, it will seem perfectly normal to you – but when speaking to influence, you are not speaking for your own benefit. Our tendency to think only about what we must do instead of what we are aiming to achieve means we focus on what we want to say rather than how it is being said. As a result, whatever your natural speaking pattern, it is not yet optimized for influencing others.

Further, as cognitive load increases – such as when answering an interview question or having to think hard about a response – our voices change in a reliable manner. Research at the University of Toulouse in France with men and women aged 19 to 48 found that as mental load increases, vocal pitch becomes higher and more unstable.[27] The study also found that our rate of speaking slows down, specifically because we take longer to pronounce vowel sounds. As a result, the pauses in our speech do not occur in places that make the message easier to understand because the rhythm is jumbled while our brains are busy processing our thoughts. In the next section we will identify what vocal characteristics you should be targeting.

How to sound interesting, confident and powerful

Voice and character in the drama department

In live theatre, both the heroes and the villains are expected to speak in voices commensurate with their noble intention or conversely, their evil schemes. Thus, it was in a doctoral dissertation for the Department of Drama at the Flinders University of South Australia that Dr Sally Nimon investigated what personality characteristics the public associated with the sound of an actor's voice.[28] To focus just on sound irrespective of the content of a message, she recorded male and female voices singing specific nonsense syllables and then modified the recordings according to three variables: Volume (loud or soft), pitch (high or low) and pacing (clear and steady vs 'breathy'* and rapid). Next, a large sample of men and women were asked to listen to those recordings and evaluate the character traits they associated with the sounds. Analysis of the results identified significant patterns in how these variables affected perceptions of the speaker. Table 9.1 represents what she found.

Louder voices attract more attention

If the volume of the TV you are watching does not meet your needs, you will automatically reach out and adjust the sound until you feel it is right. Your target audience can't do that to your voice. In many professional environments, whether in a live meeting

---

*A 'breathy' voice sounds airy, murmured or whispery. We might speak in a breathy and rapid voice when feeling excited or nervous

TABLE 9.1: Vocal features and reaction to speaker in dramatic theatre

Variable	Value	Audience Reaction to Character
Volume	Louder, projected volume (vs softer volume)	Stronger and more interesting (vs weaker and more boring)
Pitch	Lower-pitched voice (vs higher-pitched)	More confident, less stressed
Pacing and Rhythm	Steady and clear (vs breathy and rapid)	Higher status or power

Adapted from Nimon (2001)[28]

with background noise from people shuffling and coughing, an auditorium larger than your TV room, or an online meeting with people sometimes talking over each other, a louder voice attracts more attention. Theatre actors project their voices so the audience can hear them and the study we have just examined shows that these louder voices are actually perceived as more interesting. Of course, if your voice is so loud that it's perceived as shouting that will carry a negative emotional connotation to the listener. However, given the likelihood that there is more competition for auditory attention in a meeting with several people or a larger room with more space for sound dispersion, it is more likely that your regular speaking voice is softer than it should be. It will be particularly important to increase your volume when you want to make an important point and therefore need to command attention.

Lower-pitched voices inspire confidence, attract votes, and make more money

In line with Nimon's study of theatre characters, studies in evolutionary biology have identified that men and women with lower-pitched voices are perceived as more dominant by both sexes.[29,30] Although the term 'dominance' might conjure images of combative chest beating, think of dominance here as a leadership or social ranking signal that is subtly encoded in vocal signals received by the subconscious. This is exactly the interpretation that was demonstrated by British and American researchers who recorded voices saying, 'I urge you to vote for me this November' and then manipulated them into either lower-pitched or higher-pitched versions of the original voices.[31] Both men and women who listened to the recordings were more likely to vote for the lower-pitched version of reality. The team repeated this experiment within the context of leadership positions that are more often held by women (such as President of the Parent-Teacher Organization at a school) and found again that the influence of voice pitch on perceptions of leadership capacity holds for different types of leadership positions.[32] These experimental findings have also been confirmed in observations from political and management contexts. For example, an analysis of the voices of candidates from 19 televised US presidential debates across eight elections (1960 to 2000) found that the relative pitch frequency of candidates' voices accurately predicted the pattern of popular voting.[33] A study of male CEOs of almost 800 public companies found that men with deeper voices managed larger companies and made more money.[34]

Emphasis, intonation and masterful use of pauses will positively affect your audience

In addition to the volume and the pitch of a voice, the rhythm of speech is a significant factor. Professor Laura Hahn at the University of Illinois examined listener response to three different recordings of the same 300-word exert of a lecture: one with no stress on any word (i.e., monotone voice), one with emphasis on random words and one in which stress was placed to correctly enhance the meaning of the content.[35] She found that the correct emphasis enabled speakers to better understand the content (measured by their ability to recall what was said) and resulted in a more favourable evaluation of the speaker than in the other two conditions. Further, although the version with random emphasis was not well received by listeners, it was still preferred when compared with the monotone version.

Beyond simply placing emphasis on the correct words, it is important to vary your intonation to match the content of the message, just as an actor would bring a script to life. In fact, the more variation in intonation a speaker uses to ensure their expression matches their content, the greater his or her perceived charisma and liveliness.[36]

Although some studies have suggested that people who speak faster are perceived as more competent (e.g.,[37]), these older studies don't consider that today we are often communicating in highly internationalized environments in which at least some people may not speak English as their first language. In fact, people who speak quickly may speak in a more breathy, rapid voice and this was associated with lower power status in Nimon's study compared to a person speaking clearly and steadily. Consider also the typically steady and clear speech pattern of highly effective speakers such as former US president Barack Obama.

The solution to finding the right pace appears to lie in where you pause because appropriate use of pauses makes your content easier to understand. Introducing pauses between key ideas breaks your message into smaller and more manageable pieces, as I discovered personally when attending a live lecture by Stephen Hawking at Cambridge University.[38] Hawking's use of an artificial voice required him to deliver his lectures on theoretical physics at a rate of a few sentences at a time, enabling me to understand one idea before we moved on to the next. In fact, introducing a pause before a keyword or idea increases people's attention to it – shown in the result that inserting a pause between a brand message and a brand name improves people's ability to remember the brand.[39]

APPLYING THE PRINCIPLE OF EXECUTION TO INFLUENCING PEOPLE AND OUTCOMES

The review of behavioural science in this chapter identifies the crucial features in your execution that can significantly affect your influencing power by moderating people's perception of your character and your message. These are summarized in Table 9.2, which provides a checklist you can use after you have made your influencing plan, but before you go live with it.

TABLE 9.2: An Execution Checklist for your influence attempt

Execution Factor	Professional Setting for Your Influence Attempt		
	Writing job applications or important emails	A live meeting, either face-to-face or online	Giving a presentation
Factor 1: **An upright, expansive posture**	Adopt this posture while composing your message, in particular when you are trying to recall positive results you have achieved, good qualities you have demonstrated or strong examples of past events.	The benefits of the posture – in terms of boosting mood, attention and positive feelings and reducing dull, sleepy or sluggish feelings appear to hold as the position is held, at least for up to 30 minutes.	Adopt this posture both when preparing your presentation and when delivering it. Practise repetitively in front of a mirror so you can see yourself and be sure you make the right adjustments.
Factor 2: **The (simple and familiar) words you choose**	What phrases or examples will resonate emotionally or cognitively with the audience? When you have drafted the application, email or CV, re-read it and consider whether or not you can simplify your expression.	What phrases or examples will resonate emotionally or cognitively with the audience? Prepare the key contribution that you want to make to the meeting (the end-goal you wish to achieve) so that it includes these familiar words – and keep it simple.	As per Principle Eight (*End-Goal Focus*) you will have chosen a specific end-goal to achieve via your presentation. Consider the language you should use in your presentation to create resonance with the audience. What concepts are familiar to them (emotional resonance)? How can you structure your presentation so it matches their needs (cognitive resonance)?

Factor 3: Have an overall message (that brings something new)	Ensure that your overall message is stated simply at the start of the email, giving you the best chance that the receiver will read it.	Ensure that your overall message is clear and ready to be delivered during your contribution to the meeting.	Ensure your overall message is clearly stated during your presentation.
Factor 4: Practise how you use your voice out loud	N/A	Some of the discussion and interactions will be spontaneous and unpredictable but make sure you have written out and practise aloud the key statements you wish to make. As you speak out loud during practice, you find ways to improve or simplify your message. You can also practise intonation and pauses.	Practise your whole presentation out loud several times over. As you speak out loud during practice, you find ways to improve or simplify your message. You can also practise intonation and pauses.

Easier said than done

Just as with many of the tools described in this book, knowing what to do, and being able to do it, are two different pursuits. Imagine yourself sitting in a college class or a company meeting. The topic under discussion is interesting and not altogether easy (think of any meeting topics you've been involved in that fit this description). You're in the process of thinking through what has been contributed when the discussion leader asks for your input and so you contribute a few sentences to the discussion. Got that image in your head right now? Good, let's proceed.

Now I'm going to ask you to repeat what you just said, but at a higher volume, with a more projected voice, a lower pitch and a steady rate of speech that contains both appropriate pauses as well as intonation that matches the content of your statement. Do you think you can do it?

I have posed this challenge to hundreds of international business school students over the past few years and, so far, not one of them has been able to do this very effectively. That is because it is too difficult to think about **how** you are speaking when you are focused on **what** you are saying. There are two solutions to that dilemma:

1. **What you say**: Practise what you want to say out loud before you go live
2. **How you say it**: Regularly perform exercises to improve your ability to make posture, word, and voice changes easily.

Ideally, it pays to do both.

Practise the fire escape before the fire

If you have ever participated in a fire drill at a workplace, institution or perhaps at an event, you might have wondered why officials require you to physically walk through the fire escape drill, rather than just giving you an explanation of what you should do if the fire alarm went off. The answer is simple: When you have physically performed an action in the past, it becomes significantly easier to repeat that action again, even if this time around the air is filled with smoke and the sound of people's screams.

By the same reasoning, repeating exactly what you want to say out loud several times over in the comfort of your own room will make it much easier for you to replicate those statements later, even if the big boss is staring at you and someone is making a distracting noise in the corner. This paradigm applies not only to being able to repeat the specific words and the specific message that you want to say to your influence target, but also to the posture and to the vocal characteristics you adopt. In summary, when you have developed an influencing plan using any or all of the Principles from One to Eight, plan a specific practice session to focus on your execution behaviours.

Bedtime stories and other daily activities to practise intentional micro changes

Similarly, your ability to quickly adopt the posture, vocabulary and use of voice that best supports your influencing effort will be strengthened if you regularly practise switching from your relaxed, default position into the more powerful position outlined in this chapter. Just as a personal trainer might prescribe 10 minutes of strength exercises four times a week to build up your calf muscles, these sorts of exercises strengthen your 'muscle memory' for adopting an upright, expansive posture, simple words that resonate, a message that is new but not too different, and a voice that is slightly louder and lower with appropriate intonation and pauses.

From the list in Table 9.3, choose the exercises that you can most easily fit into your daily routine. Aim to practise each of the four execution factors for several minutes each, two or three times per week.

BETTER THAN YESTERDAY: USING THE PRINCIPLE OF EXECUTION TO BOOST CONFIDENCE AND PERFORMANCE

Slouching might feel comfortable, but as we have seen, adopting an upright expansive posture makes it easier for you to feel positive and to access happy thoughts. If you find yourself working long hours at a desk and starting to feel drowsy, dull

TABLE 9.3: Execution strengthening exercises for forming a routine

Execution Factor	Possible Practice Exercises
Factor 1: **An upright,** **expansive** **posture**	• Sit in a chair facing a mirror. Note the position of your head, spine, and shoulders, as well as your arms and legs. Now, consciously shift each of these aspects of your posture so that they match the ideal model described under 'Factor 1'. Hold for one minute. Relax. Repeat the exercise. • Repeat this exercise, this time sitting in a chair, side-on to a mirror. • Repeat this exercise, this time standing facing a mirror, then again standing side-on to a mirror.
Factor 2: **The (simple** **and familiar)** **words you** **choose**	• Where is it easy for you to come across complex sentences? Perhaps you have a technical textbook on your shelf, get your coffee from a shop that holds copies of *The Economist*, or regularly watch a news report. Choose one or two complex sentences and challenge yourself to find a much simpler set of words to express the same idea without changing the meaning. Perform this exercise at a specific moment in the day and repeat it four times across the week. • Repeat this exercise, considering what changes in vocabulary or terminology you would choose if your goal was to resonate with a group of kindergarteners. • Repeat this exercise, considering what changes in vocabulary or terminology you would choose if your goal was to resonate with a group of senior finance managers, or human resources professionals in a specific industry.
Factor 3: **Have an** **overall** **message** **that brings** **something** **new**	• Sit still for a moment and reflect on your last weekend or day off work. Think about all the different things you did or tried to do, who you saw and where you went from the time you woke up until the time you went to bed. Next, design two sentences that summarize all that information into a message. • Repeat this exercise after your next weekend or day off. Create a message that is like your first message, but adds a new type of information, such as how you felt at the end of the day. • As an alternative to this exercise, read a paragraph from a book, article or magazine. Now close the book or switch off the screen and summarize what you just read in two sentences. What was the message contained in that paragraph?

Factor 4:
Practise how
you use your
voice out
loud

- Listen to David Attenborough introduce himself in this YouTube clip.[40] Notice the pitch variation as he says: 'I am David Attenborough and I am 93.' Replicate his intonation while introducing yourself.
- Read a bedtime story to a younger sibling, child or relative. Aim to exaggerate the emotion and drama of the story. Use your voice to give life to characters or to render a scenario exciting or scary.
- As an alternative to this exercise, practise reading a paragraph from a newspaper, magazine or even Wikipedia as if you were an actor auditioning for a movie. Bring life and passion into the story.
- In pairs, ask your partner to say a few sentences about a subject they care about very much, or a subject that disgusts them. When they bring emotion into the topic, you will hear variation in how they use their voice. Repeat the exercise on yourself.

---

or depressed, then adopting an upright expansive position and going for a walk for as little as 13 minutes can help improve your mood.[15]

Similarly, there are many reasons why it might be hard for you to speak up in front of a group of peers or colleagues. Public speaking may cause you anxiety, but also some personality types are associated with being less likely to voice one's opinions: for example, extroverts are more likely to speak up in a group of people than are introverts. Your reluctance to speak up does not mean your ideas are any less valuable, just as the natural sound of your voice should not be a basis for judging your character, even if science shows that human brains are biased to work in these directions. Be mindful of trying to avoid such biases when assessing people with whom you interact. At the same time, having the ability to put on the physical characteristics that subtly communicate power to other members of our species will give a boost to your confidence and your performance.

ILLUSTRATION OF PRINCIPLE NINE (*EXECUTION*)
FIGURE 9

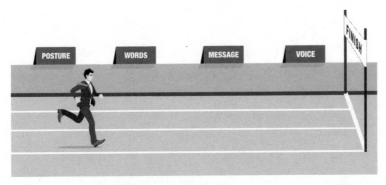

FIGURE 9: A great influencing plan needs to be executed in a manner that reinforces that influence. Like the final 100m of a race, there is work to be done on your posture, words, message, and voice.

Key takeaways

- Crucial features in your execution can significantly affect perception of your character, your trustworthiness and competence and these have a knock-on effect on your ability to influence.

- Your body posture can significantly affect your mood, confidence, and behaviour. Adopting an upright expansive posture will enable you to feel better and perform better when faced with the kind of stressful tasks that routinely occur in the workplace.

- You can influence how people perceive your message by careful choice of the specific words you use. Use simple words in place of more complex or difficult ones and choose words that resonate with the beliefs and emotions of the influence target.

- The most successful opinion-changing arguments have messages that summarize communication and provide new information but are communicated in words similar to those used by the original opinion-holder.

- Whatever your natural speaking pattern, it is not yet optimized for influencing others.

- Louder and more low-pitched voices tend to inspire confidence and attract attention. Varying your intonation in an appropriate manner makes you appear more charismatic and makes your message more memorable.

- When you have developed an influencing plan using any or all of the Principles from One to Eight, plan a specific practice session to focus on your execution behaviours and strengthen your muscle memory. This must be done in advance because it is too difficult to focus on what you are saying as well as how you are saying it in the heat of the moment.

Conclusion: What to Do Now

AM I AN EXPERT YET?

Certainly, you now know a lot more about influence at work than you did before you read this book. Nonetheless, there is practically an infinite number of ways in which our perception, decisions and behaviours are affected by biases and shortcuts. Most of the time we cannot witness these effects because they occur at a subconscious level in our brains. By the time our conscious brains become aware of the various stimuli in our environment, that data has been woven into a sensible narrative about a rational, fair, and admirable human being making very reasonable decisions. It is only through approaches such as behavioural science that we can objectively observe some of the very strange ways in which we behave as a species.

The nine principles presented in this book are just a subset of all those shortcuts, but they are particularly relevant to you as a professional seeking to have more influence. Every one of the chosen nine principles has special relevance to the workplace of the twenty-first century. As you have seen, in every chapter there are examples, exercises and advice to enable you to make the link between knowledge and application in your own working life.

THE SCIENCE-BASED REASON FOR PROVIDING YOU WITH NINE PRINCIPLES

In fact, nine is the maximum number of meaningful units of information that the brain can process easily and hold in short-term memory. You may have heard of this as Miller's Law, the

TABLE IO.I: Nine science-based principles to accelerate your career by increasing your influence over people and outcomes

People-related:	*Perception-related:*	*Behaviour-related:*
Principle One is **Status**	Principle Four is **Value Framing**	Principle Seven is **Inertia**
Principle Two is **Social Imitation**	Principle Five is **Effort**	Principle Eight is **End-Goal Focus**
Principle Three is **Affiliation**	Principle Six is **Reasoning**	Principle Nine is **Execution**

theory that we are best able to remember seven units of data, plus or minus two.[1] This means that to keep information in your working memory where it can be accessed easily, it is best to aim for no more than nine units of data. Further, remembering information also becomes easier when that information is structured into meaningful chunks. As a result, the model provided in this book includes nine principles structured into three units of three principles. Once you recite the model out loud a few times over a few days, it will become easy to remember (Table 10.1).

KNOWING IS IMPORTANT, IT'S JUST NOT THE SAME AS DOING

Knowing how to do something is not the same as being able to do it. I learned this after watching Grand Slam winner Serena Williams play tennis. Intellectually, I know what she is doing on court – but put a racket in my hand and we will quickly establish that I can't come close to doing what she does. **Yet.**

The 'yet' is important. In using this word, I choose to acknowledge two extremely powerful concepts in developing expertise. The first is **Incremental Mindset**, a perspective that helps drive successful skill development, as established by Professor Carol Dweck of Stanford University.[2,3] According to Incremental Mindset, people become more successful at improving their skills when they stop relying on natural talent and instead become determined to work for improvements. As a result, they focus on the goal of becoming better, whatever their current starting line. Progress is then made incrementally, small step by small step, from where you are now to where you want to be.

The second key concept is **Deliberate Practice**, a methodology for skill development established by Professor Anders Ericsson of Florida State University.[4,5] According to Deliberate Practice, people build sustainable skill improvement by breaking complex skills into their component pieces and then aiming to improve in these smaller pieces. A good analogy is a tennis player practising to improve in backhand instead of trying to win a game. When players aim to improve in backhand, then forehand, then serving, then volleys, their overall performance level will eventually improve. Of course, it is crucial that this deliberate practice occurs in an environment where the risks are low: you practise to improve your backhand during practice time, not during match time.

Taken together, these powerful concepts provide valuable guidelines for developing your influencing skills:

1. **Start with one exercise or one section from your favourite principle**. For example, you might choose re-writing your accomplishments using value conversion (from Principle Four: *Value Framing*) or setting a specific end-goal for your next meeting (Principle Eight: *End-Goal Focus*).

2. **Identify a low-risk situation in which you can practise it**. In other words, don't try it out during a crucial job interview; create a practice situation instead.

3. **Work at improving until you can see progress**. Expertise is not an all-or-nothing phenomenon; it is built through successive micro-improvements.

4. **When you use the new skill in a real-life situation, take the time to reflect on what went well and what you could have improved**. This is also a core element of the deliberate practice methodology that leads to successful improvement.

5. **Keep practising to improve, even when you don't get the exact outcome you expected**. As per the example of the job candidate who got a pay rise rather than a promotion

(Principle Seven: *Inertia*), you can't control all the variables – but you will eventually achieve more success by developing these skills.

The knowing/doing issue is a frequent problem in business schools and business books that aim to improve people's capability.[6] Right now you have knowledge, but the only way to build real skill is to start practising on a small but regular basis, in a safe environment. The principles you have learned are tools, just like a tennis racket is a tool. The more you practise with them, test them out for yourself and observe the results you achieve, the better you will become at using these tools.

Although we may never put the effort into practising that would be required to emulate Serena Williams, following the approach above would certainly help us become massively better at tennis. Furthermore, you do not need to be the number one expert in influence in the world, you are just aiming to have more influence over people and outcomes at work than you used to have before you learned these principles.

AM I ON MY OWN NOW?

Not at all. First, you will find a series of short, supporting videos on my YouTube Channel *Career Success Psychology*. In addition to explainer videos that refresh your memory of each principle, you will find more short videos of science-backed approaches to improving your career success.

Second, you are invited to submit a story about your experience using any of the Working with Influence principles on the website: dramandanimonpeters.com. There, you will also find some troubleshooting tips, as well as a variety of other short articles designed to help you accelerate your professional career.

Once again, I wish you good luck, success and fun while learning.

Dr Amanda Nimon-Peters
Professor of Leadership
Hult International Business School

References

Principle One: Status

1. Milgram, S. (1963). 'Behavioural Study of Obedience', *The Journal of Abnormal and Social Psychology*, 67(4), 371–378. https://doi.org/10.1037/h0040525

2. Milgram, S. (1974). *Obedience to Authority: An Experimental View*, Harper & Row: New York.

3. Doliński, D., Grzyb, T., Folwarczny, M., Grzybała, P., Krzyszycha, K., Martynowska, K. & Trojanowski, J. (2017). 'Would You Deliver an Electric Shock in 2015? Obedience in the Experimental Paradigm Developed by Stanley Milgram in the 50 Years Following the Original Studies', *Social Psychological and Personality Science*, 8(8), 927–933. https://doi.org/10.1177/1948550617693060

4. Blass, T. (1999). 'The Milgram Paradigm After 35 Years: Some Things We Now Know About Obedience to Authority', *Journal of Applied Social Psychology*, 29(5), 955–978. https://doi.org/10.1111/j.1559-1816.1999.tb00134.x

5. Eagly, A.H. (1978). 'Sex Differences in Influenceability', *Psychological Bulletin*, 85(1), 86–116. https://doi.org/10.1037/0033-2909.85.1.86

6. Sheridan, C.L. & King, R.G. (1972). 'Obedience to Authority with an Authentic Victim', *Proceedings of the Annual Convention of the American Psychological Association*, 165–166. https://doi.org/10.1037/e465522008-083

7. Caspar, E.A., Christensen, J.F., Cleeremans, A. & Haggard, P. (2016). 'Coercion Changes the Sense of Agency in the Human Brain', *Current Biology*, 26(5), 585–592. https://doi.org/10.1016/j.cub.2015.12.067

8. Abbott, A. (25 February 2016). 'How the Brain Reacts to Orders: Modern Spin on Iconic Milgram Experiments Suggests that People Obeying Commands Feel Less Responsible for Actions', *Nature, 530*(7591), 394–395.

9. Berger, J., Cohen, B.P. & Zelditch, M. (1972). 'Status Characteristics and Social Interaction', *American Sociological Review, 37*(3), 241. https://doi.org/10.2307/2093465

10. Correll, S.J. & Ridgeway, C.L. (2006). 'Expectation States Theory'. In J. DeLamater (Ed.), *Handbook of Social Psychology* (Ser. Handbooks of Sociology and Social Research, pp. 29–51). Springer, Boston MA.

11. Webster, M. & Slattery Walker, L. (2016). 'The Theories of Status Characteristics and Expectation States'. In *Handbook of Contemporary Sociological Theory* (pp. 321–342). Springer: Cham.

12. Brashears, M.E. (2008). 'Sex, Society, and Association: A Cross-national Examination of Status Construction Theory', *Social Psychology Quarterly, 71*(1), 72–85. https://doi.org/10.1177 /019027250807100108

13. Huberman, B.A., Loch, C.H. & Önçüler, A. (2004). 'Status As a Valued Resource', *Social Psychology Quarterly, 67*(1), 103–114. https://doi.org/10.1177/019027250406700109

14. Koski J., Xie, H. & Olson, I.R. (2015). 'Understanding Social Hierarchies: The Neural and Psychological Foundations of Status Perception', *Social Neuroscience, 10*(5), 527–550. doi:10.1080/17470 919.2015.1013223

15. Berger, J. & Fişek, M.H. (2006). 'Diffuse Status Characteristics and the Spread of Status Value: A Formal Theory', *American Journal of Sociology, 111*(4), 1038–1079. https://doi.org/10.1086/498633

16. Olivola, C.Y., Funk, F. & Todorov, A. (2014). 'Social Attributions from Faces Bias Human Choices', *Trends in Cognitive Sciences, 18*(11), 566–570.

17. Webster, M. & Foschi, M. (1988). *Status Generalization: New Theory and Research,* Stanford University Press.

18. Peck, B.M. & Conner, S. (2011). 'Talking with Me or Talking at Me? The Impact of Status Characteristics on Doctor-Patient Interaction', *Sociological Perspectives, 54*(4), 547–567. https://doi.org /10.1525/sop.2011.54.4.547

19. Stulp, G., Buunk, A.P., Verhulst, S. & Pollet, T.V. (2015). 'Human Height Is Positively Related to Interpersonal Dominance in Dyadic Interactions', *PLOS ONE, 10*(2). https://doi.org/10.1371/journal .pone.0117860

20. Verhulst, B., Lodge, M. & Lavine, H. (2010). 'The Attractiveness Halo: Why Some Candidates are Perceived More Favourably than Others', *Journal of Nonverbal Behaviour, 34*, 111–117. https://doi.org/10.1007/s10919-009-0084-z

21. Berggren, N., Jordahl, H. & Poutvaara, P. (2010). 'The Looks of a Winner: Beauty and Electoral Success', *Journal of Public Economics, 94*(1–2), 8–15. https://doi.org/10.1016/j.jpubeco.2009.11.002

22. Rosette, A.S., Leonardelli, G.J. & Phillips, K.W. (2008). 'The White Standard: Racial Bias in Leader Categorization', *Journal of Applied Psychology, 93*(4), 758–777. https://doi.org/10.1037/0021-9010.93.4.758

23. Feller, T. (2010). 'What the Literature Tells Us About the Jury Foreperson', *The Jury Expert, 22*, 42–51.

24. Pazhoohi, F., Silva, C., Lamas, J., Mouta, S., Santos, J. & Arantes, J. (2018). 'The Effect of Height and Shoulder-to-hip Ratio on Interpersonal Space in Virtual Environment', *Psychological Research, 83*(6), 1184–1193. https://doi.org/10.1007/s00426-017-0968-1

25. Batres, C., Re, D.E. & Perrett, D.I. (2015). 'Influence of Perceived Height, Masculinity, and Age on Each Other and on Perceptions of Dominance in Male Faces', *Perception, 44*(11), 1293–1309. https://doi.org/10.1177/0301006615596898

26. Antonakis, J. & Eubanks, D.L. (2017). 'Looking Leadership in the Face', *Current Directions in Psychological Science, 26*(3), 270–275. https://doi.org/10.1177/0963721417705888

27. Re, D.E., Hunter, D.W., Coetzee, V., Tiddeman, B.P., Xiao, D., DeBruine, L.M. & Perrett, D.I. (2013). 'Looking Like a Leader–Facial Shape Predicts Perceived Height and Leadership Ability', *PLoS ONE, 8*(12). https://doi.org/10.1371/journal.pone.0080957

28. Marschan-Piekkari, R., Welch, D.E. & Welch, L.S. (2015). *Language in International Business: The Multilingual Reality of Global Business Expansion*, Edward Elgar.

29. Järlström, M., Piekkari, R., Pilke, N. & Turpeinen, H. (2020). 'Perceptions of Language (Mis)fit at a Multilingual Workplace: The Case of the University of Vaasa', *Language Perceptions and Practices in Multilingual Universities*, 293–322. https://doi.org/10.1007/978-3-030-38755-6_12

30. Ritter, A. & Yoder, J.D. (2004). 'Gender Differences in Leader Emergence Persist Even for Dominant Women: An Updated Confirmation of Role Congruity Theory', *Psychology of Women Quarterly, 28*(3), 187–193. doi:10.1111/j.1471-6402.2004.00135.x

31. Brunell, A.B., Gentry, W.A., Campbell, W.K., Hoffman, B.J., Kuhnert, K.W. & DeMarree, K.G. (2008). 'Leader Emergence: The Case of the Narcissistic Leader', *Personality and Social Psychology Bulletin, 34*(12), 1663–1676. https://doi.org/10.1177 /0146167208324101

32. Reuben, E., Rey-Biel, P., Sapienza, P. & Zingales, L. (2012). 'The Emergence of Male Leadership in Competitive Environments', *Journal of Economic Behaviour & Organization, 83*(1), 111–117. https://doi.org/10.1016/j.jebo.2011.06.016

33. Chamorro-Premuzic, T. (2013). 'Why Do So Many Incompetent Men Become Leaders?', *Harvard Business Review Digital Articles, 8/22/2013*, 2–4.

34. Banaji, M.R. & Greenwald, A.G. (2016). *Blindspot: Hidden Biases of Good People*, Bantam.

35. Steele, C. (2011). *Whistling Vivaldi: And Other Clues to How Stereotypes Affect Us*, W.W. Norton.

36. John, L.K. (2021). 'Savvy Self-promotion', *Harvard Business Review, 99*(3), 145–148.

37. Sezer, O., Gino, F. & Norton, M.I. (2018). 'Humblebragging: A Distinct—and Ineffective—Self-presentation Strategy', *Journal of Personality and Social Psychology, 114*(1), 52–74. https://doi.org/10 .1037/pspi0000108

38. Gurung, R.A., Brickner, M., Leet, M. & Punke, E. (2017). 'Dressing "In Code": Clothing Rules, Propriety, and Perceptions', *The Journal of Social Psychology, 158*(5), 553–557. https://doi.org/10 .1080/00224545.2017.1393383

39. Howlett, N., Pine, K., Orakçıoğlu, I. & Fletcher, B. (2013). 'The Influence of Clothing on First Impressions', *Journal of Fashion Marketing and Management: An International Journal, 17*(1), 38–48. https://doi.org/10.1108/13612021311305128

Principle Two: Social Imitation

1. McDonald, R.I. & Crandall, C.S. (2015). 'Social Norms and Social Influence', *Current Opinion in Behavioural Sciences, 3*, 147–151.

2. Higgs, S. & Ruddock, H. (2020). 'Social Influences on Eating', *Handbook of Eating and Drinking: Interdisciplinary Perspectives*, 277–291.

3. Robinson, S.L. & O'Leary-Kelly, A.M. (1998). 'Monkey See, Monkey Do: The Influence of Work Groups on the Antisocial

Behaviour of Employees', *Academy of Management Journal*, *41*(6), 658–672. https://doi.org/10.5465/256963

4. Nook, E.C. & Zaki, J. (2015). 'Social Norms Shift Behavioural and Neural Responses to Foods', *Journal of Cognitive Neuroscience*, *27*(7), 1412–1426. https://doi.org/10.1162/jocn_a_00795

5. Persson E., Barrafrem, K., Meunier, A. & Tinghög, G. (2019). 'The Effect of Decision Fatigue on Surgeons' Clinical Decision Making', *Health Economics, 28*(10), 1194–1203. doi:10.1002/hec.3933

6. Danziger, S., Levav, J. & Avnaim-Pesso, L. (2011). 'Extraneous Factors in Judicial Decisions', *Proceedings of the National Academy of Sciences, 108*(17), 6889–6892. doi:10.1073/pnas.1018033108

7. Massara, F., Melara, R.D. & Liu, S.S. (2013). 'Impulse Versus Opportunistic Purchasing During a Grocery Shopping Experience', *Marketing Letters, 25*(4), 361–372. doi:10.1007/s11002-013-9255-0

8. Huh, Y.E., Vosgerau, J. & Morewedge, C.K. (2014). 'Social Defaults: Observed Choices Become Choice Defaults', *Journal of Consumer Research, 41*(3), 746–760. doi:10.1086/677315

9. Reese, G., Loew, K. & Steffgen, G. (2014). 'A Towel Less: Social Norms Enhance Pro-Environmental Behaviour in Hotels', *The Journal of Social Psychology, 154*(2), 97–100. doi:10.1080/00224545.2013.855623

10. Thomas J., Ursell, A., Robinson, E.L., Aveyard, P., Jebb, S.A., Herman, C.P. & Higgs, S. (2017). 'Using a Descriptive Social Norm to Increase Vegetable Selection in Workplace Restaurant Settings', *Health Psychology, 36*(11), 1026–1033. doi:10.1037/hea0000478

11. Handgraaf M., Van Lidth De Jeude, M.A. & Appelt, K.C. (2013). 'Public Praise vs. Private Pay: Effects of Rewards on Energy Conservation in the Workplace', *Ecological Economics, 86*, 86–92. doi:10.1016/j.ecolecon.2012.11.008

12. Munch, E. (2020). 'Social Norms on Working Hours and Peak Times in Public Transport', *Time & Society*, 1–30. doi:10.1177/0961463x20905478

13. Keenan, K., Saburova, L., Bobrova, N., Elbourne, D., Ashwin, S. & Leon, D.A. (2015). 'Social Factors Influencing Russian Male Alcohol Use Over the Life Course: A Qualitative Study Investigating Age Based Social Norms, Masculinity, and Workplace Context', *Plos One, 10*(11). doi:10.1371/journal.pone.0142993

14. Neighbors, C., Labrie, J.W., Hummer, J.F., Lewis, M.A., Lee, C.M., Desai, S. & Larimer, M.E. (2010). 'Group Identification as a Moderator of the Relationship Between Perceived Social Norms and

Alcohol Consumption', *Psychology of Addictive Behaviours, 24*(3), 522–528. doi:10.1037/a0019944

15. Egebark J. & Ekström, M. (2017). 'Liking What Others "Like": Using Facebook to Identify Determinants of Conformity', *Experimental Economics, 21*(4), 793–814. doi:10.1007/s10683-017-9552-1

16. Jun, Y., Meng, R. & Johar, G.V. (2017). 'Perceived Social Presence Reduces Fact-checking', *Proceedings of the National Academy of Sciences, 114*(23), 5976–5981. doi:10.1073/pnas.1700175114

17. Robertson, L. (19 November 2014). 'That Chain E-mail Your Friend Sent to You Is (Likely) Bogus. Seriously', Retrieved from: https://www.factcheck.org/2008/03/that-chain-e-mail-your-friend-sent-to-you-is-likely-bogus-seriously/

18. Shao, C., Ciampaglia, G.L., Varol, O., Flammini, A. & Menczer, F. (2017). 'The Spread of Misinformation by Social Bots'. arXiv preprint arXiv:1707.07592

19. Bergström A. & Belfrage, M.J. (2018). 'News in Social Media: Incidental Consumption and the Role of Opinion Leaders', *Digital Journalism, 6*(5), 583–598. doi:10.1080/21670811.2018.1423625

20. Asch, S. (1951). 'Effects of Group Pressure Upon the Modification and Distortion of Judgments'. In H. Guetzkow (Ed.), *Groups, Leadership and Men: Research in Human Relations* (pp. 177–190), Carnegie Press.

21. Amir, T. (1984). 'The Asch Conformity Effect: A Study in Kuwait', *Social Behaviour and Personality: An International Journal, 12*(2), 187–190. doi:10.2224/sbp.1984.12.2.187

22. Larsen, K.S. (1991). 'The Asch Conformity Experiment: Replication and Transhistorical Comparisons'. In James W. Neuliep (Ed.), *Replication Research in the Social Sciences* (pp. 151–156). Newbury Park, CA: Sage.

23. Lisciandra C., Postma-Nilsenová, M. & Colombo, M. (2013). 'Conformorality: A Study on Group Conditioning of Normative Judgment', *Review of Philosophy and Psychology, 4*(4), 751–764. doi:10.1007/s13164-013-0161-4

24. Festinger, L. (1954). 'A Theory of Social Comparison Processes', *Human Relations, 7*(2), 117–140. doi:10.1177/001872675400700202

25. Chan, E. & Briers, B. (2019). 'It's the End of the Competition: When Social Comparison is Not Always Motivating for Goal Achievement', *Journal of Consumer Research, 46*(2), 351–370. doi:10.1093/jcr/ucy075

26. Davis D., Jivet, I., Kizilcec, R.F., Chen, G., Hauff, C. & Houben, G. (2017). 'Follow the Successful Crowd: Raising MOOC Completion Rates through Social Comparison at Scale', *Proceedings of the Seventh International Learning Analytics & Knowledge Conference.* doi:10.1145/3027385.3027411

27. Nolan, J.M., Schultz, P.W., Cialdini, R.B., Goldstein, N.J. & Griskevicius, V. (2008). 'Normative Social Influence is Underdetected', *Personality and Social Psychology Bulletin, 34(7)*, 913–923. doi:10.1177/0146167208316691

28. Cialdini, R.B. (2007). 'Descriptive Social Norms as Underappreciated Sources of Social Control', *Psychometrika, 72(2)*, 263–268. doi:10.1007/s11336-006-1560-6

29. Goodall, J. (1971). *In the Shadow of Man*, Houghton Mifflin Harcourt: New York.

30. Asch, S.E. (1956). 'Studies of Independence and Conformity: I. A Minority of One Against a Unanimous Majority', *Psychological Monographs: General and Applied, 70(9)*, 1–70.

31. Burris, E.R. (2011). 'The Risks and Rewards of Speaking Up: Managerial Responses to Employee Voice', *Academy of Management Journal, 55(4)*, 851–875. doi:10.5465/amj.2010.0562

32. Hulin, C., Fitzgerald, L. & Drasgow, F. (1996). 'Organizational Influences on Sexual Harassment'. In M.S. Stockdale (Ed.), *Women and Work: A Research and Policy Series, Volume 5: Sexual harassment in the workplace: Perspectives, frontiers, and response strategies* (pp. 127–150). Thousand Oaks, CA: SAGE Publications, Inc. doi: 10.4135/9781483327280.n7

33. National Academies of Sciences, Engineering, and Medicine (2018). *Sexual Harassment of Women: Climate, Culture, and Consequences in Academic Sciences, Engineering, and Medicine*, Washington, DC: The National Academies Press. doi: https://doi.org/10.17226/24994

34. Peck, E. (16 June 2018). 'Want to End Sexual Harassment? Landmark Study Finds Ousting "Bad Men" Isn't Enough' [Editorial]. Retrieved from https://www.huffpost.com/entry/sexual -harassment-ousting-bad-men_n_5b23f8c3e4b0f9178a9cd6f5

Principle Three: Affiliation

1. Casciaro, T. & Sousa Lobo, M. (2005). 'Competent Jerks, Lovable Fools, and the Formation of Social Networks', *Harvard Business Review, 83(6)*, 92–99.

2. Casciaro, T. & Sousa Lobo, M. (2008). 'When Competence is Irrelevant: The Role of Interpersonal Affect in Task-related Ties', *Administrative Science Quarterly, 53*(4), 655–684. doi:10.2189/asqu.53.4.655

3. Singh, R. & Tor, X.L. (2008). 'The Relative Effects of Competence and Likability on Interpersonal Attraction', *The Journal of Social Psychology, 148*(2), 253–256. doi:10.3200/socp.148.2.253-256

4. Lykourentzou, I., Kraut, R.E. & Dow, S.P. (2017). 'Team Dating Leads to Better Online Ad Hoc Collaborations', *Proceedings of the 2017 ACM Conference on Computer Supported Cooperative Work and Social Computing*, 2330–2343. doi:10.1145/2998181.2998322

5. Maslow, A.H. (1943). 'A Theory of Human Motivation', *Psychological Review, 50*(4), 370–396. https://doi.org/10.1037/h0054346

6. McClelland, D. (1987). 'The Need for Affiliation'. In D. McClelland (Ed.), *Human Motivation* (pp. 346–347), Cambridge: Cambridge University Press.

7. Leroy, T., Christophe, V., Delelis, G., Corbeil, M. & Nandrino, J. (2010). 'Social Affiliation as a Way to Socially Regulate Emotions: Effects of Others' Situational and Emotional Similarities', *Current Research in Social Psychology, 16*(1).

8. Tajfel, H. (1974). 'Social Identity and Intergroup Behaviour', *Social Science Information, 13*(2), 65–93. doi:10.1177/053901847401300204

9. Tajfel, H. (1970). 'Experiments in Intergroup Discrimination', *Scientific American, 223*(5), 96–102. doi:10.1038/scientificamerican1170-96

10. Molenberghs, P. & Louis, W.R. (2018). 'Insights From fMRI Studies Into Ingroup Bias', *Frontiers in Psychology*, 9. https://doi.org/10.3389/fpsyg.2018.01868

11. Molenberghs, P., Halász, V., Mattingley, J.B., Vanman, E.J. & Cunnington, R. (2012). 'Seeing is Believing: Neural Mechanisms of Action-perception are Biased by Team Membership', *Human Brain Mapping, 34*(9), 2055–2068. https://doi.org/10.1002/hbm.22044

12. Tajfel, H., Billig, M.G., Bundy, R.P. & Flament, C. (1971). 'Social Categorization and Intergroup Behaviour', *European Journal of Social Psychology, 1*(2), 149–178. doi:10.1002/ejsp.2420010202

13. Frank, M. & Gilovich, T. (1988). 'The Dark Side of Self- and Social Perception: Black Uniforms and Aggression in Professional

Sports', *Journal of Personality and Social Psychology*, *54*(1), 74–85. doi:10.1037/0022-3514.54.1.74

14. Schulz, A., Wirth, W. & Müller, P. (2018). 'We are the People and You are Fake News: A Social Identity Approach to Populist Citizens' False Consensus and Hostile Media Perceptions', *Communication Research*, *47*(2), 201–226. https://doi.org/10.1177 /0093650218794854

15. Jin, K. & Baillargeon, R. (2017). 'Infants Possess an Abstract Expectation of Ingroup Support', *Proceedings of the National Academy of Sciences*, *114*(31), 8199–8204. doi:10.1073/ pnas.1706286114

16 Aronson, E. & Worchel, P. (1966). 'Similarity Versus Liking as Determinants of Interpersonal Attractiveness', *Psychonomic Science*, *5*(4), 157–158. doi:10.3758/bf03328329

17. Izuma, K., Saito, D.N. & Sadato, N. (2008). 'Processing of Social and Monetary Rewards in the Human Striatum', *Neuron*, *58*(2), 284–294. https://doi.org/10.1016/j.neuron.2008.03.020

18. Gordon, R. (1996). 'Impact of Ingratiation on Judgments and Evaluations: A Meta-analytic Investigation', *Journal of Personality and Social Psychology*, *71*(1), 54–70. doi:10.1037/0022-3514.71.1.54

19. Cortes, K. & Wood, J.V. (2019). 'How was Your Day? Conveying Care, But Under the Radar, for People Lower in Trust', *Journal of Experimental Social Psychology*, *83*, 11–22. doi:10.1016/j. jesp.2019.03.003

20. Russell, J.A., Brock, S. & Rudisill, M.E. (2019). 'Recognizing the Impact of Bias in Faculty Recruitment, Retention, and Advancement Processes', *Kinesiology Review*, *8*(4), 291–295. https:// doi.org/10.1123/kr.2019-0043

21. Trainer, T., Taylor, J.R. & Stanton, C.J. (2020). 'Choosing the Best Robot for the Job: Affinity Bias in Human-robot Interaction', *Social Robotics*, 490–501. https://doi.org/10.1007/978-3-030 -62056-1_41

22. Chatman, C.M. & von Hippel, W. (2001). 'Attributional Mediation of In-group Bias', *Journal of Experimental Social Psychology*, *37*(3), 267–272. https://doi.org/10.1006/jesp.2000.1457

23. Castelli, L., Tomelleri, S. & Zogmaister, C. (2008). 'Implicit Ingroup Metafavouritism: Subtle Preference for Ingroup Members Displaying Ingroup Bias', *Personality and Social Psychology Bulletin*, *34*(6), 807–818. https://doi.org/10.1177/0146167208315210

24. Garner, R. (2005). 'What's in a Name? Persuasion Perhaps', *Journal of Consumer Psychology, 15*(2), 108–116. doi:10.1207/s15327663jcp1502_3

25. Pulles, N. & Hartman, P. (2017). 'Likeability and Its Effect on Outcomes of Interpersonal Interaction', *Industrial Marketing Management, 66*, 56–63. doi:10.1016/j.indmarman.2017.06.008

26. Jayanti, R.K. & Whipple, T.W. (2008). 'Like Me … Like Me Not: The Role of Physician Likability on Service Evaluations', *Journal of Marketing Theory and Practice, 16*(1), 79–86. doi:10.2753/mtp1069-6679160106

27. Mills, J. (1971). 'Effect on Opinion Change of the Communicator's Liking for the Audience He Addressed', *Psychonomic Science, 25*(6), 335–337. doi:10.3758/bf03335897

28. Lin, Y.-T., Hung, T.-W. & Huang, L. T.-L. (2020). 'Engineering Equity: How AI Can Help Reduce the Harm of Implicit Bias', *Philosophy & Technology.* https://doi.org/10.1007/s13347-020-00406-7

29. Vélez, N., Bridgers, S. & Gweon, H. (2019). 'The Rare Preference Effect: Statistical Information Influences Social Affiliation Judgments', *Cognition, 192*, 103994. https://doi.org/10.1016/j.cognition.2019.06.006

30. Berman, B. (2016). 'Referral Marketing: Harnessing the Power of Your Customers', *Business Horizons, 59*(1), 19–28. https://doi.org/10.1016/j.bushor.2015.08.001

31. Heilman, M.E., Wallen, A.S., Fuchs, D. & Tamkins, M.M. (2004). 'Penalties for Success: Reactions to Women Who Succeed at Male Gender-typed Tasks', *Journal of Applied Psychology, 89*(3), 416–427. https://doi.org/10.1037/0021-9010.89.3.416

32. El-Alayli, A., Hansen-Brown, A.A. & Ceynar, M. (2018). 'Dancing Backwards in High Heels: Female Professors Experience More Work Demands and Special Favour Requests, Particularly From Academically Entitled Students', *Sex Roles, 79*(3–4), 136–150. https://doi.org/10.1007/s11199-017-0872-6

33. Weger, H., Castle, G.R. & Emmett, M.C. (2010). 'Active Listening in Peer Interviews: The Influence of Message Paraphrasing on Perceptions of Listening Skill', *International Journal of Listening, 24*(1), 34–49. https://doi.org/10.1080/10904010903466311

34. Mae, L., Carlston, D.E. & Skowronski, J.J. (1999). 'Spontaneous Trait Transference to Familiar Communications: Is a Little Knowledge a Dangerous Thing?', *Journal of Personality and Social Psychology, 77*(2), 233–246. https://doi.org/10.1037/0022-3514.77.2.233

35. Hatfield, E., Cacioppo, J.T. & Rapson, R.L. (1993). 'Emotional Contagion', *Current Directions in Psychological Science*, *2*(3), 96–100. https://doi.org/10.1111/1467-8721.ep10770953

PRINCIPLE FOUR: VALUE FRAMING

1. Zimmermann, M. (1986). 'Neurophysiology of Sensory Systems'. In *Fundamentals of Sensory Physiology* (pp. 68–116). Springer, Berlin, Heidelberg.
2. Thomadsen, R., Rooderkerk, R.P., Amir, O., Arora, N., Bollinger, B., Hansen, K. & Sudhir, K. (2018). 'How Context Affects Choice', *Customer Needs and Solutions*, *5*(1–2), 3–14.
3. Davtyan, D. & Cunningham, I. (2017). 'An Investigation of Brand Placement Effects on Brand Attitudes and Purchase Intentions: Brand Placements Versus TV Commercials', *Journal of Business Research*, *70*, 160–167. doi:10.1016/j.jbusres.2016.08.023
4. Lubow, R.E., Rifkin, B. & Alek, M. (1976). 'The Context Effect: The Relationship Between Stimulus Preexposure and Environmental Preexposure Determines Subsequent Learning', *Journal of Experimental Psychology: Animal Behaviour Processes*, *2*(1), 38–47. doi:10.1037/0097-7403.2.1.38
5. Wendt, S., Strunk, K.S., Heinze, J., Roider, A. & Czaczkes, T.J. (2019). 'Positive and Negative Incentive Contrasts Lead to Relative Value Perception in Ants', *ELife Sciences*, *8*. doi:10.7554/elife.45450.030
6. Calbi, M., Heimann, K., Barratt, D., Siri, F., Umiltà, M.A. & Gallese, V. (2017). 'How Context Influences Our Perception of Emotional Faces: A Behavioural Study on the Kuleshov Effect', *Frontiers in Psychology*, *8*. https://doi.org/10.3389/fpsyg.2017.01684
7. Wyer, R. (2007). 'Principles of Mental Representation'. In A. Kruglanski & E. Higgins (Eds.), *Social Psychology: Handbook of Basic Principles* (pp. 285–307), The Guilford Press.
8. Goldberg, M.E. & Gorn, G.J. (1987). 'Happy and Sad TV Programmes: How They Affect Reactions to Commercials', *Journal of Consumer Research*, *14*(3), 387. https://doi.org/10.1086/209122
9. Urquhart, A., Wake, N. & Nimon-Peters, A. (2017). 'The Effects of Teaching Style on Student Recall', *Proceedings of EurOMA 2017*. Retrieved from http://euroma2017.org/wp-content/uploads/2017/07/Euroma-2017-Schedule-V6-final.pdf
10. Bower, G. (1981). 'Mood and Memory', *American Psychologist*, *36*(2), 129–148. doi:https://web.stanford.edu/~gbower/1981/Mood_Memory_in_American_Psychologist.pdf

11. Isen, A.M., Daubman, K.A. & Nowicki, G.P. (1987). 'Positive Affect Facilitates Creative Problem Solving', *Journal of Personality and Social Psychology, 52*(6), 1122–1131. doi:10.1037/0022-3514.52.6.1122

12. Mikkelson, D. (14 November 2014). 'Daughter's Letter Home: A College Student Sends Her Parents a Letter Filled With Disastrous News'. https://www.snopes.com/fact-check/letter-go-2/

13. Cialdini, R., Vincent, J.E., Lewis, S.K., Catalan, J., Wheeler, D. & Darby, B.L. (1975). 'Reciprocal Concessions Procedure for Inducing Compliance: The Door-in-the-face Technique', *Journal of Personality and Social Psychology, 31*(2), 206–215. doi:10.1037/h0076284

14. Medvec, V.H., Madey, S.F. & Gilovich, T. (2004). 'When Less is More: Counterfactual Thinking and Satisfaction Among Olympic Medalists', *Social Cognition*, 579–588. https://doi.org/10.4324/9780203496398-36

15. Kahneman, D. & Tversky, A. (1979). 'Prospect Theory: An Analysis of Decision Under Risk', *Econometrica, 47*(2), 263. https://doi.org/10.2307/1914185

16. Pras, B. (1978). 'Explaining Consumer Decision Making Through Evaluation Process Models', *Marketing*, 145–161. https://doi.org/10.1007/978-3-322-93787-2_8

17. Boyce, J., Brown, G.D. & Moore, S.C. (2010). 'Money and Happiness', *Psychological Science, 21*(4), 471–475. doi:10.1177/0956797610362671

18. Brosnan, S.F. & Waal, F.B. (2003). 'Monkeys Reject Unequal Pay', *Nature, 425*(6955), 297–299. doi:10.1038/nature01963

19. Brooks, M.E., Guidroz, A.M. & Chakrabarti, M. (2009). 'Distinction Bias in Applicant Reactions to Using Diversity Information in Selection', *International Journal of Selection and Assessment, 17*(4), 377–390. https://doi.org/10.1111/j.1468-2389.2009.00480.x

20. Hsee, C.K. & Zhang, J. (2004). 'Distinction Bias: Misprediction and Mischoice Due to Joint Evaluation', *Journal of Personality and Social Psychology, 86*(5), 680–695. https://doi.org/10.1037/0022-3514.86.5.680

21. Parker, S., Bascom, J., Rabinovitz, B. & Zellner, D. (2008). 'Positive and Negative Hedonic Contrast with Musical Stimuli', *Psychology of Aesthetics, Creativity, and the Arts, 2*(3), 171–174. doi:10.1037/1931-3896.2.3.171

22. Simcock, N., Macgregor, S., Catney, P., Dobson, A., Ormerod, M., Robinson, Z. & Hall, S.M. (2014). 'Factors Influencing Perceptions of Domestic Energy Information: Content, Source

and Process', *Energy Policy*, *65*, 455–464. doi:10.1016/j.
enpol.2013.10.038

23. TEDx Talks. (20 March 2013). 'Three Myths of Behaviour Change
– What You Think You Know That You Don't'. Retrieved from
https://www.youtube.com/watch?v=l5d8GW6GdRo

24. Dunn, D., Saville, B., Baker, S. & Marek, P. (2013). 'Evidence-
based Teaching: Tools and Techniques That Promote Learning in the
Psychology Classroom: Evidence-based Teaching', *Australian Journal
of Psychology*, *65*(1), 5–13.

25. Funk, C. & Kennedy, B. (2016). 'Public Knowledge about Science
has a Limited Tie to People's Beliefs about Climate Change and
Climate Scientists'. In C. Funk & B. Kennedy (Authors), *The Politics
of Climate* (pp. 68–75), Pew Research Centre. doi:https://www.
pewresearch.org/science/2016/10/04/public-knowledge-about-
science-has-a-limited-tie-to-peoples-beliefs-about-climate-change-
and-climate-scientists/

26. Webster, R., Brooks, S., Smith, L., Woodland, L., Wessely, S. &
Rubin, J. (2020). 'How to Improve Adherence with Quarantine:
Rapid Review of the Evidence', *Public Health*, *182*, 163–169.
doi:10.31219/osf.io/c5pz8

27. Procter & Gamble. (n.d.). 'Policies and Practices: Purpose, Values,
& Principles', Retrieved 25 January 2021 from https://en-ae.pg.com
/policies-and-practices/purpose-values-and-principles/

28. Hirsch, J.B., Kang, S.K. & Bodenhausen, G.V. (2012). 'Personalized
Persuasion: Tailoring Persuasive Appeals to Recipients' Personality
Traits', *Psychological Science*, Vol. 23, No. 6, pp. 578–581.

29. Vohs, K., Baumeister, R., Twenge, J., Schmeichel, B., Tice, D. &
Crocker, J. (2005). 'Decision Fatigue Exhausts Self-Regulatory
Resources – But So Does Accommodating to Unchosen Alternative'.
Retrieved from: https://web.archive.org/web/20111004053220
/https://www.chicagobooth.edu/research/workshops/marketing/
archive/WorkshopPapers/vohs.pdf

30. Bloom, L. & Bloom, C. (14 December 2017). 'Reframing: The
Transformative Power of Suffering', Retrieved 25 January 2021 from
https://www.psychologytoday.com/us/blog/stronger-the-broken
-places/201712/reframing

PRINCIPLE FIVE: EFFORT

1. Zipf, G.K. (1949). *Human Behaviour and the Principle of Least Effort:
An Introduction to Human Ecology*, Cambridge, MA: Addison-Wesley.

2. Kanwal, J., Smith, K., Culbertson, J. & Kirby, S. (2017). 'Zipf's Law of Abbreviation and the Principle of Least Effort: Language Users Optimise a Miniature Lexicon for Efficient Communication', *Cognition, 165*, 45–52. doi:10.1016/j.cognition.2017.05.001

3. Barnett, A. & Doubleday, Z. (2020). 'The Growth of Acronyms in the Scientific Literature', *ELife, 9*. https://doi.org/10.7554/elife.60080

4. Kuhn, I.F. (2007). 'Abbreviations and Acronyms in Healthcare: When Shorter Isn't Sweeter', *Pediatric Nursing, 33*(5), 392–398.

5. Mirabela, P.A. & Ariana, S.M. (2009). 'The Use of Acronyms and Initialisms in Business English', *Annals of Faculty of Economics, 1*(1), 557–562.

6. Shipton, C., Blinkhorn, J., Breeze, P.S., Cuthbertson, P., Drake, N., Groucutt, H.S. & Petraglia, M.D. (2018). 'Acheulean Technology and Landscape Use at Dawadmi, Central Arabia', *Plos One, 13*(7). doi:10.1371/journal.pone.0200497

7. Australian National University (10 August 2018). 'Laziness Helped Lead to Extinction of Homo Erectus', *ScienceDaily*. Retrieved 27 July 2020 from www.sciencedaily.com/releases/2018/08/180810091542.htm

8. Guy, S.J., Curtis, S., Lin, M.C. & Manocha, D. (2012). 'Least-effort Trajectories Lead to Emergent Crowd Behaviours', *Physical Review E, 85*(1). doi:10.1103/physreve.85.016110

9. Ahmed, K. (9 October 2017). 'Richard Thaler and the Economics of How We Live'. Retrieved from https://www.bbc.com/news/business-41550434

10. Wansink, B. & Kim, J. (2005). 'Bad Popcorn in Big Buckets: Portion Size Can Influence Intake as Much as Taste', *Journal of Nutrition Education and Behaviour, 37*(5), 242–245. doi:10.1016/s1499-4046(06)60278-9

11. Hagura, N., Haggard, P. & Diedrichsen, J. (2017). 'Perceptual Decisions are Biased By the Cost to Act', *ELife, 6*. doi:10.7554/elife.18422

12. Kahneman, D. (2011). *Thinking, Fast and Slow*, New York: Farrar, Straus and Giroux.

13. Ninio, A. & Kahneman, D. (1974). 'Reaction Time in Focused and in Divided Attention', *Journal of Experimental Psychology, 103*(3), 394–399. doi:10.1037/h0037202

14. Baymard Institute (21 September 2016). 'New E-Commerce Checkout Research – Why 68 per cent of Users Abandon Their

Cart'. Retrieved from: https://baymard.com/blog/ecommerce
-checkout-usability-report-and-benchmark

15. Bates, M. (2005). 'An Introduction to Metatheories, Theories and
    Models'. In K.E. Fisher, S. Erdelez & L. McKechnie (Eds.), *Theories
    of Information Behaviour* (pp. 1–24). Medford, NJ: *Information
    Today*.

16. Schwartz, B., Ben-Haim, Y. & Dacso, C. (2010). 'What Makes
    a Good Decision? Robust Satisficing as a Normative Standard
    of Rational Decision Making', *Journal for the Theory of Social
    Behaviour, 41*(2), 209–227. https://doi.org/10.1111/j.1468-5914
    .2010.00450.x

17. Rusz, D., Le Pelley, M.E., Kompier, M.A., Mait, L. & Bijleveld,
    E. (2020). 'Reward-driven Distraction: A Meta-analysis',
    Psychological Bulletin, 146(10), 872–899. https://doi.org/10.1037/
    bul0000296

18. Flesch, R. (1948). 'A New Readability Yardstick', *Journal of Applied
    Psychology, 32*(3), 221–233. https://doi.org/10.1037/h0057532

19. Fry, E. (1990). 'A Readability Formula for Short Passages', *Journal of
    Reading, 33*(8), 594–597.

20. Baker, W. (1994). 'How to Produce and Communicate Structured
    Text', *Technical Communication, 41*(3), 456–466.

21. Yukl, G. & Falbe, C.M. (1990). 'Influence Tactics and Objectives
    in Upward, Downward, and Lateral Influence Attempts', *Journal
    of Applied Psychology, 75*(2), 132–140. doi:10.1037/0021-
    9010.75.2.132

22. Falbe, C. & Yukl, G. (1992). 'Consequences for Managers of Using
    Single Influence Tactics and Combinations of Tactics', *Academy of
    Management Journal, 35*(3), 638–652. doi:10.5465/256490

23. Lee, S., Han, S., Cheong, M., Kim, S.L. & Yun, S. (2017).
    'How Do I Get My Way? A Meta-analytic Review of Research
    on Influence Tactics', *The Leadership Quarterly, 28*(1), 210–228.
    doi:10.1016/j.leaqua.2016.11.001

24. Giesbrecht, B. (2015). 'Pomodoro Technique for Time
    Management', *White Papers, 19*. Retrieved from https://
    digitalcommons.unomaha.edu/nbdcwhitepapers/19

Principle Six: Reasoning

1. Langer, E.J., Blank, A. & Chanowitz, B. (1978). 'The Mindlessness
   of Ostensibly Thoughtful Action: The Role of "Placebic"

Information in Interpersonal Interaction', *Journal of Personality and Social Psychology, 36*(6), 635–642. doi:10.1037/0022-3514.36.6.635

2. Higgins, C.A., Judge, T.A. & Ferris, G.R. (2002). 'Influence Tactics and Work Outcomes: A Meta-analysis', *Journal of Organizational Behaviour, 24*(1), 89–106. https://doi.org/10.1002/job.181

3. Lee, S., Han, S., Cheong, M., Kim, S.L. & Yun, S. (2017). 'How Do I Get My Way? A Meta-analytic Review of Research on Influence Tactics', *The Leadership Quarterly, 28*(1), 210–228. https://doi.org/10.1016/j.leaqua.2016.11.001

4. Manning, T. (2012). 'The Art of Successful Influence: Matching Influence Strategies and Styles to the Context', *Industrial and Commercial Training, 44*(1), 26–34. https://doi.org/10.1108/00197851211193390

5. Epitropaki, O. & Martin, R. (2013). 'Transformational–transactional Leadership and Upward Influence: The Role of Relative Leader–Member Exchanges (RLMX) and Perceived Organizational Support (POS)', *The Leadership Quarterly, 24*(2), 299–315. https://doi.org/10.1016/j.leaqua.2012.11.007

6. Bohns, V.K. & Flynn, F.J. (2010). '"Why Didn't You Just Ask?" Underestimating the Discomfort of Help-Seeking', *Journal of Experimental Social Psychology, 46*(2), 402–409. https://doi.org/10.1016/j.jesp.2009.12.015

7. Bohns, V.K. & Flynn, F.J. (2013). 'Underestimating Our Influence Over Others at Work', *Research in Organizational Behaviour, 33*, 97–112. https://doi.org/10.1016/j.riob.2013.10.002

8. Bohns, V.K., Handgraaf, M.J.J., Sun, J., Aaldering, H., Mao, C. & Logg, J. (2011). 'Are Social Prediction Errors Universal? Predicting Compliance With a Direct Request Across Cultures', *Journal of Experimental Social Psychology, 47*(3), 676–680. https://doi.org/10.1016/j.jesp.2011.01.001

9. Curtis, V. (2004). 'The Art of Persuasion', *New Scientist, 184*(2478), 21–21.

10. Bolino, G. (2012). 'Power of Persuasion', *Utility Week*, 24–25 January.

11. Schwartz, D., Bruine de Bruin, W., Fischhoff, B. & Lave, L. (2015). 'Advertising Energy Saving Programmes: The Potential Environmental Cost of Emphasizing Monetary Savings', *Journal of Experimental Psychology: Applied, 21*(2), 158–166. https://doi.org/10.1037/xap0000042

12. Bélanger, J., Haines, V.Y. & Bernard, M. (2017). 'Human Resources Professionals and the Cost/Benefit Argument: Rational Persuasion in Action in Municipal Organizations', *The International Journal of Human Resource Management*, *29*(16), 2431–2454. https://doi.org /10.1080/09585192.2016.1277362

13. Falbe, C.M. & Yukl, G. (1992). 'Consequences for Managers of Using Single Influence Tactics and Combinations of Tactics', *Academy of Management Journal*, *35*(3), 638–652. https://doi.org/10 .5465/256490

14. Zukier, H. (1982). 'The Dilution Effect: The Role of the Correlation and the Dispersion of Predictor Variables in the Use of Nondiagnostic Information', *Journal of Personality and Social Psychology*, *43*(6), 1163–1174. https://doi.org/10.1037/0022-3514 .43.6.1163

15. Johnson, E.J. & Tversky, A. (1983). 'Affect, Generalization, and the Perception of Risk', *Journal of Personality and Social Psychology*, *45*(1), 20–31. https://doi.org/10.1037/0022-3514.45.1.20

16. Isen, A.M. & Shalker, T.E. (1982). 'The Effect of Feeling State on Evaluation of Positive, Neutral, and Negative Stimuli: When You "Accentuate the Positive," Do You "Eliminate the Negative"?', *Social Psychology Quarterly*, *45*(1), 58. https://doi.org/10.2307/3033676

17. Greifeneder, R., Bless, H. & Pham, M.T. (2010). 'When Do People Rely on Affective and Cognitive Feelings in Judgment? A review', *Personality and Social Psychology Review*, *15*(2), 107–141. https://doi .org/10.1177/1088868310367640

18. Bunner, J., Prem, R. & Korunka, C. (2019). 'How Do Safety Engineers Improve Their Job Performance? The Roles of Influence Tactics, Expert Power, and Management Support', *Employee Relations: The International Journal*, *42*(2), 381–397. https://doi.org /10.1108/er-04-2018-0120

19. Wang, W., Qiu, L., Kim, D. & Benbasat, I. (2016). 'Effects of Rational and Social Appeals of Online Recommendation Agents on Cognition- and Affect-based Trust', *Decision Support Systems*, *86*, 48–60. https://doi.org/10.1016/j.dss.2016.03.007

20. Langer, E.J. & Piper, A.I. (1987). 'The Prevention of Mindlessness', *Journal of Personality and Social Psychology*, *53*(2), 280–287. https:// doi.org/10.1037/0022-3514.53.2.280

21. Curtis, V.A., Garbrah-Aidoo, N. & Scott, B. (2007). 'Ethics in Public Health Research', *American Journal of Public Health*, *97*(4), 634–641. https://doi.org/10.2105/ajph.2006.090589

22. Motoki, K., Suzuki, S., Kawashima, R. & Sugiura, M. (2020). 'A Combination of Self-reported Data and Social-related Neural Measures Forecasts Viral Marketing Success on Social Media', *Journal of Interactive Marketing*, *52*, 99–117. https://doi.org/10.1016/j.intmar.2020.06.003

23. Ellis, D. & Maikoo, M. (2018). 'South African Children's Influence Tactics: What Works and When? *Young Consumers*, *19*(4), 432–449. https://doi.org/10.1108/yc-02-2018-00778

Principle Seven: Inertia

1. Little, J. (2016). *The Warrior Within: The Philosophies of Bruce Lee*, Chartwell Books.

2. Goodreads. (n.d.). *Quotes by Bruce Lee*. Goodreads. https://www.goodreads.com/quotes/29138-be-like-water-making-its-way-through-cracks-do-not

3. Clarke, H. (2013). 'Context, Communication and Commiseration: Psychological and Practical Considerations in Change Management', *Perspectives: Policy and Practice in Higher Education*, *17*(1), 30–36.

4. Salari, N., Hosseinian-Far, A., Jalali, R., Vaisi-Raygani, A., Rasoulpoor, S., Mohammadi, M. & Khaledi-Paveh, B. (2020). 'Prevalence of Stress, Anxiety, Depression Among the General Population During the COVID-19 Pandemic: A Systematic Review and Meta-analysis', *Globalization and Health*, *16*(1). https://doi.org/10.1186/s12992-020-00589-w

5. Anholt, R.R.H. (2020). 'Evolution of Epistatic Networks and the Genetic Basis of Innate Behaviours', *Trends in Genetics*, *36*(1), 24–29. https://doi.org/10.1016/j.tig.2019.10.005

6. Hutton, S.B. & Nolte, S. (2011). 'The Effect of Gaze Cues on Attention to Print Advertisements', *Applied Cognitive Psychology*, *25*(6), 887–892. https://doi.org/10.1002/acp.1763

7. Sajjacholapunt, P. & Ball, L.J. (2014). 'The Influence of Banner Advertisements on Attention and Memory: Human Faces with Averted Gaze Can Enhance Advertising Effectiveness', *Frontiers in Psychology*, *5*. https://doi.org/10.3389/fpsyg.2014.00166

8. Schank, R.C. & Abelson, R.P. (1977). *Scripts, Plans, Goals and Understanding: an Inquiry into Human Knowledge Structures*, Hillsdale: Laurence Erlbaum Associates.

9. Gioia, D.A. & Poole, P.P. (1984). 'Scripts in Organizational Behaviour', *The Academy of Management Review*, *9*(3), 449. https://doi.org/10.2307/258285

10. Barnett, D., Bauer, A., Bell, S., Elliott, N., Haski, H., Barkley, E.
    & Mackiewicz, K. (2007). 'Preschool Intervention Scripts: Lessons
    from 20 years of Research and Practice', *The Journal of Speech and
    Language Pathology – Applied Behaviour Analysis*, *2*(2), 158–181.
    https://doi.org/10.1037/h0100216

11. Cooper, J.O., Heron, T.E. & Heward, W.L. (1987). Chapter 15:
    Behaviour Chains. In *Applied Behaviour Analysis*, Upper Saddle
    River, NJ: Prentice-Hall.

12. Ouellette, J.A. & Wood, W. (1998). 'Habit and Intention in
    Everyday Life: The Multiple Processes By Which Past Behaviour
    Predicts Future Behaviour', *Psychological Bulletin*, *124*(1), 54–74.
    https://doi.org/10.1037/0033-2909.124.1.54

13. Thrailkill, E.A. & Bouton, M.E. (2017). 'Factors That Influence
    the Persistence and Relapse of Discriminated Behaviour Chains',
    Behavioural Processes, *141*, 3–10. https://doi.org/10.1016/j.beproc
    .2017.04.009

14. Ochsner, K.N., Knierim, K., Ludlow, D.H., Hanelin, J.,
    Ramachandran, T., Glover, G. & Mackey, S.C. (2004). 'Reflecting
    Upon Feelings: An fMRI Study of Neural Systems Supporting the
    Attribution of Emotion to Self and Other', *Journal of Cognitive
    Neuroscience*, *16*(10), 1746–1772. https://doi.org/10.1162
    /0898929042947829

15. Frith, C.D. & Frith, U. (2006). 'How We Predict What Other
    People are Going to Do', *Brain Research*, *1079*(1), 36–46. https://doi
    .org/10.1016/j.brainres.2005.12.126

16. Balcetis, E. & Dunning, D. (2013). 'Considering the Situation:
    Why People are Better Social Psychologists Than Self-psychologists',
    Self and Identity, *12*(1), 1–15.

17. Helzer, E.G. & Dunning, D. (2012). 'Why and When Peer
    Prediction is Superior to Self-prediction: The Weight Given to
    Future Aspiration Versus Past Achievement', *Journal of Personality
    and Social Psychology*, *103*(1), 38–53.

18. Poon, C.S.K., Koehler, D.J. & Buehler, R. (2014). 'On the
    Psychology of Self-prediction: Consideration of Situational Barriers
    to Intended Actions', *Judgment and Decision Making*, *9*(3), 207–225.

19. Lindqvist, A. & Björklund, F. (2018). 'How Predictions of
    Economic Behaviour are Affected by the Socio-economic Status of
    the Target Person', *The Journal of Social Psychology*, *158*(3), 361–378.
    https://doi.org/10.1080/00224545.2017.1357527

20. Ponsi, G., Panasiti, M.S., Scandola, M. & Aglioti, S.M. (2016).
    'Influence of Warmth and Competence on the Promotion of

Safe In-group Selection: Stereotype Content Model and Social Categorization of Faces', *Quarterly Journal of Experimental Psychology*, *69*(8), 1464–1479. https://doi.org/10.1080/17470218.2015.1084339

21. Fiske, S.T. (2018). 'Stereotype Content: Warmth and Competence Endure', *Current Directions in Psychological Science*, *27*(2), 67–73. https://doi.org/10.1177/0963721417738825

22. Phelps, E.A., O'Connor, K.J., Cunningham, W.A., Funayama, E.S., Gatenby, J.C., Gore, J.C. & Banaji, M.R. (2000). 'Performance on Indirect Measures of Race Evaluation Predicts Amygdala Activation', *Journal of Cognitive Neuroscience. 12*(5), 729–738.

23. Nimon-Peters, A. (9 July 2020). 'Your Life in a Woman's Hands', Retrieved from: https://www.hult.edu/blog/your-life-in-a-womans-hands/

24. *The Economist.* (10 April 2021). 'Design Bias is Harmful, and in Some Cases May Be Lethal'. https://www.economist.com/leaders/2021/04/10/design-bias-is-harmful-and-in-some-cases-may-be-lethal.

Principle Eight: End-Goal Focus

1. Mischel, W., Ebbesen, E.B. & Raskoff Zeiss, A. (1972). 'Cognitive and Attentional Mechanisms in Delay of Gratification', *Journal of Personality and Social Psychology*, *21*(2), 204–218. https://doi.org/10.1037/h0032198

2. Mischel, W. & Ebbesen, E.B. (1970). 'Attention in Delay of Gratification', *Journal of Personality and Social Psychology*, *16*(2), 329–337. https://doi.org/10.1037/h0029815

3. Lamm, B., Keller, H., Teiser, J., Gudi, H., Yovsi, R.D., Freitag, C., Poloczek, S., Fassbender, I., Suhrke, J., Teubert, M., Vöhringer, I., Knopf, M., Schwarzer, G. & Lohaus, A. (2017). 'Waiting for the Second Treat: Developing Culture-specific Modes of Self-regulation', *Child Development*, *89*(3). https://doi.org/10.1111/cdev.12847

4. Da Silva, S., Moreira, B. & Da Costa, N. (2014). '2D:4D Digit Ratio Predicts Delay of Gratification in Preschoolers', *PLoS ONE*, *9*(12). https://doi.org/10.1371/journal.pone.0114394

5. Beran, M.J. & Evans, T.A. (2006). 'Maintenance of Delay of Gratification By Four Chimpanzees (Pan Troglodytes): The Effects of Delayed Reward Visibility, Experimenter Presence, and Extended Delay Intervals', *Behavioural Processes*, *73*(3), 315–324. https://doi.org/10.1016/j.beproc.2006.07.005

6. Schnell, A.K., Boeckle, M., Rivera, M., Clayton, N.S. &
    Hanlon, R.T. (2021). 'Cuttlefish Exert Self-control in a Delay of
    Gratification Task', *Proceedings of the Royal Society B: Biological
    Sciences*, *288*(1946), 20203161 https://doi.org/10.1098/rspb
    .2020.3161

7. Mischel, W., Shoda, Y. & Peake, P.K. (1988). 'The Nature of
    Adolescent Competencies Predicted by Preschool Delay of
    Gratification', *Journal of Personality and Social Psychology*, *54*(4),
    687–696. https://doi.org/10.1037/0022-3514.54.4.687

8. Mischel, W., Shoda, Y. & Rodriguez, M. (1989). 'Delay of
    Gratification in Children', *Science*, *244*(4907), 933–938. https://doi
    .org/10.1126/science.2658056

9. Duckworth, A.L. (2011). 'The Significance of Self-control',
    *Proceedings of the National Academy of Sciences of the United States of
    America*, *108*(7), 2639–2640.

10. Moffitt, T.E., Arseneault, L., Belsky, D., Dickson, N., Hancox, R.J.,
    Harrington, H., Houts, R., Poulton, R., Roberts, B.W., Ross, S.,
    Sears, M.R., Thomson, W.M. & Caspi, A. (2011). 'A Gradient of
    Childhood Self-control Predicts Health, Wealth, and Public Safety',
    Proceedings of the National Academy of Sciences, *108*(7), 2693–2698.
    https://doi.org/10.1073/pnas.1010076108

11. Romer, D., Duckworth, A.L., Sznitman, S. & Park, S. (2010).
    'Can Adolescents Learn Self-control? Delay of Gratification in the
    Development of Control Over Risk Taking', *Prevention Science*,
    11(3), 319–330. https://doi.org/10.1007/s11121-010-0171-8

12. Benjamin, D.J., Laibson, D., Mischel, W., Peake, P.K., Shoda, Y.,
    Wellsjo, A.S. & Wilson, N.L. (2020). 'Predicting Mid-life Capital
    Formation with Pre-school Delay of Gratification and Life-course
    Measures of Self-regulation', *Journal of Economic Behaviour &
    Organization*, *179*, 743–756. https://doi.org/10.1016/j.jebo.2019
    .08.016

13. Watts, T.W., Duncan, G.J. & Quan, H. (2018). 'Revisiting the
    Marshmallow Test: A Conceptual Replication Investigating Links
    Between Early Delay of Gratification and Later Outcomes',
    Psychological Science, *29*(7), 1159–1177. https://doi.org/10.1177
    /0956797618761661

14. Amar, M., Ariely, D., Ayal, S., Cryder, C.E. & Rick, S.I. (2011).
    'Winning the Battle but Losing the War: The Psychology of Debt
    Management', *Journal of Marketing Research*, *48*(SPL). https://doi
    .org/10.1509/jmkr.48.spl.s38

15. Baumeister, R.F. (2002). 'Yielding to Temptation: Self-control Failure, Impulsive Purchasing, and Consumer Behaviour', *Journal of Consumer Research*, *28*(4), 670–676. https://doi.org/10.1086/338209

16. Fiebelkorn, I.C., Pinsk, M.A. & Kastner, S. (2018). 'A Dynamic Interplay Within the Frontoparietal Network Underlies Rhythmic Spatial Attention', *Neuron*, *99*(4). https://doi.org/10.1016/j.neuron.2018.07.038

17. Simons, D.J. & Chabris, C.F. (1999). 'Gorillas in Our Midst: Sustained Inattentional Blindness for Dynamic Events', *Perception*, *28*(9), 1059–1074. https://doi.org/10.1068/p2952

18. Murphy, G. & Greene, C.M. (2016). 'Perceptual Load Induces Inattentional Blindness in Drivers', *Applied Cognitive Psychology*, *30*(3), 479–483. https://doi.org/10.1002/acp.3216

19. Immordino-Yang, M.H. (2016). *Emotions, Learning, and the Brain: Exploring the Educational Implications of Affective Neuroscience*, p. 32. W.W. Norton & Company.

20. Nimon-Peters, A. (22 October 2020). *Why Learner 'Happiness' is Essential From the Outset, Especially During a Pandemic*, TrainingZone. https://www.trainingzone.co.uk/deliver/training/why-learner-happiness-is-essential-from-the-outset-especially-during-a-pandemic

21. Urquhart, A., Wake, N. & Nimon-Peters, A.J. (2017). 'The Effects of Teaching Style on Student Recall'. In: *Proceedings of EurOMA 2017*. Retrieved from: https://doi.org/http://euroma2017.eiasm.org/userfiles/HKIGIKI_GDFJMK_JT7XYoWS.pdf

22. Middlebrooks, C.D., Kerr, T. & Castel, A.D. (2017). 'Selectively Distracted: Divided Attention and Memory for Important Information', *Psychological Science*, *28*(8), 1103–1115. https://doi.org/10.1177/0956797617702502

23. Rusz, D., Le Pelley, M.E., Kompier, M.A., Mait, L. & Bijleveld, E. (2020). 'Reward-driven Distraction: A Meta-analysis', *Psychological Bulletin*, *146*(10), 872–899. https://doi.org/10.1037/bul0000296

24. Horberry, T., Osborne, R. & Young, K. (2019). 'Pedestrian Smartphone Distraction: Prevalence and Potential Severity', *Transportation Research Part F: Traffic Psychology and Behaviour*, *60*, 515–523. https://doi.org/10.1016/j.trf.2018.11.011

25. Festinger, L. (1954). 'A Theory of Social Comparison Processes', *Human Relations*, *7*(2), 117–140. https://doi.org/10.1177/001872675400700202

26. Raff, K. & Siming, L. (2019). 'Knighthoods, Damehoods, and CEO Behaviour', *Journal of Corporate Finance*, *59*, 302–319. https://doi.org/10.1016/j.jcorpfin.2016.10.004

27. Burton, D. (1989). 'Winning Isn't Everything: Examining the Impact of Performance Goals on Collegiate Swimmers' Cognitions and Performance', *The Sport Psychologist, 3*(2), 105–132. https://doi.org/10.1123/tsp.3.2.105

28. Kim, S., Park, Y.A. & Niu, Q. (2016). 'Micro-break Activities at Work to Recover From Daily Work Demands', *Journal of Organizational Behaviour, 38*(1), 28–44. https://doi.org/10.1002/job.2109

29. Kohli, C., Leuthesser, L. & Suri, R. (2007). 'Got Slogan? Guidelines for Creating Effective Slogans', *Business Horizons, 50*(5), 415–422. https://doi.org/10.1016/j.bushor.2007.05.002

30. Mendoza, J.S., Pody, B.C., Lee, S., Kim, M. & McDonough, I.M. (2018). 'The Effect of Cellphones on Attention and Learning: The Influences of Time, Distraction, and Nomophobia', *Computers in Human Behaviour, 86*, 52–60. https://doi.org/10.1016/j.chb.2018.04.027

31. Killingsworth, M.A. & Gilbert, D.T. (2010). 'A Wandering Mind is an Unhappy Mind', *Science, 330*(6006), 932–932. https://doi.org/10.1126/science.1192439

32. Kirschner, P.A. & De Bruyckere, P. (2017). 'The Myths of the Digital Native and the Multitasker', *Teaching and Teacher Education, 67*, 135–142. https://doi.org/10.1016/j.tate.2017.06.001

PRINCIPLE NINE: THE LAST 100M

1. Akehurst, L., Köhnken, G., Vrij, A. & Bull, R. (1996). 'Lay Persons' and Police Officers' Beliefs Regarding Deceptive Behaviour', *Applied Cognitive Psychology, 10*(6), 461–471.

2. Desmarais, S. & Yarney, D. (2004). 'Judgements of Deception and Accuracy of Performance in Eyewitness Testimony', *The Canadian Journal of Police and Security Services, 2*(3), 13–22.

3. Silver, I., Mellers, B.A. & Tetlock, P.E. (2021). 'Wise Teamwork: Collective Confidence Calibration Predicts the Effectiveness of Group Discussion', *Journal of Experimental Social Psychology, 96*, 104157. https://doi.org/10.1016/j.jesp.2021.104157

4. Carney, D.R., Cuddy, A.J.C. & Yap, A.J. (2010). 'Power Posing: Brief Nonverbal Displays Affect Neuroendocrine Levels and Risk Tolerance', *Psychological Science, 21*(10), 1363–1368. https://doi.org/10.1177/0956797610383437

5. TED (1 November 2012). *Your Body Language May Shape Who You Are | Amy Cuddy* [Video]. YouTube. https://www.youtube.com/watch?v=Ks-_Mh1QhMc

6. Cuddy, A.J., Wilmuth, C.A., Yap, A.J. & Carney, D.R. (2015). 'Preparatory Power Posing Affects Nonverbal Presence and Job Interview Performance', *Journal of Applied Psychology, 100*(4), 1286–1295. https://doi.org/10.1037/a0038543

7. Bohns, V.K. & Wiltermuth, S.S. (2012). 'It Hurts When I Do This (Or You Do That): Posture and Pain Tolerance', *Journal of Experimental Social Psychology, 48*(1), 341–345. https://doi.org/10.1016/j.jesp.2011.05.022

8. Ranehill, E., Dreber, A., Johannesson, M., Leiberg, S., Sul, S. & Weber, R.A. (2015). 'Assessing the Robustness of Power Posing: No Effect on Hormones and Risk Tolerance in a Large Sample of Men and Women', *Psychological Science, 26*(5), 653–656. https://doi.org/10.1177/0956797614553946

9. Briñol, P., Petty, R.E. & Wagner, B. (2009). 'Body Posture Effects on Self-evaluation: A Self-validation Approach', *European Journal of Social Psychology, 39*(6), 1053–1064. https://doi.org/10.1002/ejsp.607

10. Körner, R., Köhler, H. & Schütz, A. (2020). 'Powerful and Confident Children Through Expansive Body Postures? A Preregistered Study of Fourth Graders', *School Psychology International, 41*(4), 315–330. https://doi.org/10.1177/0143034320912306

11. Elkjær, E., Mikkelsen, M.B., Michalak, J., Mennin, D.S. & O'Toole, M.S. (2020). 'Expansive and Contractive Postures and Movement: A Systematic Review and Meta-analysis of the Effect of Motor Displays on Affective and Behavioural Responses', *Perspectives on Psychological Science*, 174569162091935. https://doi.org/10.1177/1745691620919358

12. Wilson, V.E. & Peper, E. (2004). 'The Effects of Upright and Slumped Postures on the Recall of Positive and Negative Thoughts', *Applied Psychophysiology and Biofeedback, 29*(3), 189–195. https://doi.org/10.1023/b:apbi.0000039057.32963.34

13. Nair, S., Sagar, M., Sollers, J., Consedine, N. & Broadbent, E. (2015). 'Do Slumped and Upright Postures Affect Stress Responses? A Randomized Trial', *Health Psychology, 34*(6), 632–641. https://doi.org/10.1037/hea0000146

14. Hackford, J., Mackey, A. & Broadbent, E. (2019). 'The Effects of Walking Posture on Affective and Physiological States During Stress', *Journal of Behaviour Therapy and Experimental Psychiatry, 62*, 80–87. https://doi.org/10.1016/j.jbtep.2018.09.004

15. Rennung, M., Blum, J. & Göritz, A.S. (2016). 'To Strike a Pose: No Stereotype Backlash for Power Posing Women', *Frontiers in Psychology*, 7. https://doi.org/10.3389/fpsyg.2016.01463

16. Vacharkulksemsuk, T., Reit, E., Khambatta, P., Eastwick, P.W., Finkel, E.J. & Carney, D.R. (2016). 'Dominant, Open Nonverbal Displays are Attractive at Zero-acquaintance', *Proceedings of the National Academy of Sciences*, *113*(15), 4009–4014. https://doi.org/10.1073/pnas.1508932113

17. Gronau, Q.F., van Erp, S., Heck, D.W., Cesario, J., Jonas, K. & Wagenmakers, E.-J. (2017). 'A Bayesian Model-averaged Meta-analysis of the Power Pose Effect With Informed and Default Priors: The Case of Felt Power'. https://doi.org/10.31222/osf.io/heamz

18. Körner, R., Petersen, L.-E. & Schütz, A. (2019). 'Do Expansive or Contractive Body Postures Affect Feelings of Self-worth? High Power Poses Impact State Self-esteem', *Current Psychology*. https://doi.org/10.1007/s12144-019-00371-1

19. Elsbach, K.D. & Elofson, G. (2000). 'How the Packaging of Decision Explanations Affects Perceptions of Trustworthiness', *Academy of Management Journal*, *43*(1), 80–89. https://doi.org/10.5465/1556387

20. Lockwood, C., Giorgi, S. & Glynn, M.A. (2018). 'How to Do Things With Words': Mechanisms Bridging Language and Action in Management Research', *Journal of Management*, *45*(1), 7–34. https://doi.org/10.1177/0149206318777599

21. Snow, D.A. & Benford, R.D. (1988). 'Ideology, Frame Resonance, and Participant Mobilization', *International Social Movement Research*, *1*(1), 197–217.

22. Giorgi, S. (2017). 'The Mind and Heart of Resonance: The Role of Cognition and Emotions in Frame Effectiveness', *Journal of Management Studies*, *54*(5), 711–738. https://doi.org/10.1111/joms.12278

23. Giorgi, S. & Weber, K. (2015). 'Marks of Distinction: Framing and Audience Appreciation in the Context of Investment Advice', *Administrative Science Quarterly*, *60*(2), 333–367. https://doi.org/10.1177/0001839215571125

24. Heath, R., Brandt, D. & Nairn, A. (2006). 'Brand Relationships: Strengthened by Emotion, Weakened by Attention', *Journal of Advertising Research*, *46*(4), 410–419. https://doi.org/10.2501/s002184990606048x

25. Kohli, C., Leuthesser, L. & Suri, R. (2007). 'Got Slogan? Guidelines for Creating Effective Slogans', *Business Horizons*, *50*(5), 415–422. https://doi.org/10.1016/j.bushor.2007.05.002

26. Tan, C., Niculae, V., Danescu-Niculescu-Mizil, C. & Lee, L. (2016). 'Winning Arguments: Interaction Dynamics and Persuasion Strategies in Good-faith Online Discussions', *Proceedings of the 25th International Conference on World Wide Web*. https://doi.org/10.1145 /2872427.2883081

27. Boyer, S., Paubel, P.-V., Ruiz, R., El Yagoubi, R. & Daurat, A. (2018). 'Human Voice as a Measure of Mental Load Level', *Journal of Speech, Language, and Hearing Research*, 61(11), 2722–2734. https://doi.org/10.1044/2018_jslhr-s-18-0066

28. Nimon, S.M. (2001). *An Investigation Into the Influence of Non-linguistic Vocal Elements on Readings of Theatrical Character* (dissertation). Doctoral dissertation, Flinders University of South Australia, Department of Drama.

29. Borkowska, B. & Pawlowski, B. (2011). 'Female Voice Frequency in the Context of Dominance and Attractiveness Perception', *Animal Behaviour*, 82(1), 55–59. https://doi.org/10.1016/j.anbehav.2011.03 .024

30. Wolff, S.E. & Puts, D.A. (2010). 'Vocal Masculinity is a Robust Dominance Signal in Men', *Behavioural Ecology and Sociobiology*, 64(10), 1673–1683. https://doi.org/10.1007/s00265-010-0981-5

31. Klofstad, C.A., Anderson, R.C. & Peters, S. (2012). 'Sounds Like a Winner: Voice Pitch Influences Perception of Leadership Capacity in Both Men and Women', *Proceedings of the Royal Society B: Biological Sciences*, 279(1738), 2698–2704. https://doi.org/10.1098/rspb.2012 .0311

32. Anderson, R.C. & Klofstad, C.A. (2012). 'Preference for Leaders with Masculine Voices Holds in the Case of Feminine Leadership Roles', *PLoS ONE*, 7(12). https://doi.org/10.1371/journal.pone .0051216

33. Gregory, S.W. & Gallagher, T.J. (2002). 'Spectral Analysis of Candidates' Nonverbal Vocal Communication: Predicting U.S. Presidential Election Outcomes', *Social Psychology Quarterly*, 65(3), 298–308. https://doi.org/10.2307/3090125

34. Mayew, W.J., Parsons, C.A. & Venkatachalam, M. (2013). 'Voice Pitch and the Labor Market Success of Male Chief Executive Officers', *Evolution and Human Behaviour*, 34(4), 243–248. https:// doi.org/10.1016/j.evolhumbehav.2013.03.001

35. Hahn, L.D. (2004). 'Primary Stress and Intelligibility: Research to Motivate the Teaching of Suprasegmentals', *TESOL Quarterly*, 38(2), 201. https://doi.org/10.2307/3588378

36. Hincks, R. & Edlund, J. (2009). 'Promoting Increased Pitch Variation in Oral Presentations with Transient Visual Feedback', *Language Learning & Technology*, *13*(3), 32–50.

37. Apple, W., Streeter, L.A. & Krauss, R.M. (1979). 'Effects of Pitch and Speech Rate on Personal Attributions', *Journal of Personality and Social Psychology*, *37*(5), 715–727. https://doi.org/10.1037/0022-3514.37.5.715

38. Nimon-Peters, A.J. [Career Success Psychology]. (27 October 2020). *Success Psychology Microlearning with Arabic Subtitles* [Video]. YouTube. https://youtu.be/980LnZmBz5I

39. Mantonakis, A. (2011). 'A Brief Pause Between a Tagline and Brand Increases Brand Name Recognition and Preference', *Applied Cognitive Psychology*, *26*(1), 61–69. https://doi.org/10.1002/acp.1797

40. Netflix. (23 September 2020). *David Attenborough: A Life on Our Planet | Official Trailer | Netflix* [Video]. YouTube. https://www.youtube.com/watch?v=64R2MYUt394

Conclusion

1. Miller, G.A. (1956). 'The Magical Number Seven, Plus or Minus Two: Some Limits on Our Capacity for Processing Information', *Psychological Review*, *63*(2), 81–97. https://doi.org/10.1037/h0043158

2. Dweck, C.S. (2008). *Mindset: The New Psychology of Success*, Ballantine Books.

3. Nimon-Peters, A.J. (1 October 2020). *The Psychology of Success (Incremental Mindset Theory) [Video]*. Career Success Psychology. Retrieved from: https://youtu.be/hJrUoj8QTao

4. Ericsson, K.A., Krampe, R.T. & Tesch-Römer, C. (1993). 'The Role of Deliberate Practice in the Acquisition of Expert Performance', *Psychological Review*, *100*(3), 363–406. https://doi.org/10.1037/0033-295x.100.3.363

5. Nimon-Peters, A.J. (13 October 2020). *Techniques for Developing Expertise: Deliberate Practice [Video]*. Career Success Psychology. Retrieved from: https://youtu.be/8rru52ilDUg

6. TEDx. (10 October 2017). *Do Business Schools Develop Leadership? Not Often | Amanda Nimon-Peters* [Video]. YouTube. https://www.youtube.com/watch?v=AVxFSpx400Q

Index